Good Magic

Good Magic

MARINA MEDICI

PRENTICE
HALL
PRESS

New York • London • Toronto • Sydney • Tokyo • Singapore

Prentice Hall Press

15 Columbus Circle
New York, New York 10023

Text Copyright © 1988 by Marina Medici
Original illustrations Copyright © 1988 by Labyrinth Publishing S.A.

Good Magic was produced by
Labyrinth Publishing S.A. Switzerland
All rights reserved
including the right of reproduction
in whole or in part in any form

Originally published in Great Britain in 1988
by Macmillan London Limited
PRENTICE HALL PRESS and colophon are registered
trademarks of Simon & Schuster Inc.

Library of Congress No. 89-42503
ISBN 0-13-360314-8

Art direction and design by Carmen Strider
Photography by Alessandro Saragosa
Printed and bound in Spain by Cronion S.A., Barcelona
Color separation by Fotolito Toscana, Florence, Italy
10 9 8 7 6 5 4 3 2
First **Prentice Hall Press** Edition 1989

Contents

Preface

Whether skeptical or accepting, man has always been fascinated by magic. It has a hold on us, and whether we know it or not it is part of us — we are magical beings.

In the beginning, primitive man had no trouble feeling the magic of existence; he could not resort to a developed intellect to see into the mechanics of nature and his connection to nature's basic forces was unquestioned because these forces spoke directly to his unconscious without having to pass through the filter of a knowledgeable mind. He felt the forces in himself and around him.

"Certainly anyone living by hunting in a wild country could not help knowing that there is great power in fear and in love. Animals can be hypnotized by fear, and can be driven to fantastic achievements by passion."

Robin Skelton

Man recognized these powers and learned to use them. The shaman or witch doctor of the native tribe, for example, was highly respected and held a position of authority. Man's chief needs were to produce good crops, make good hunting and good fishing, increase his flocks and herds and produce many children to make the tribe strong. It became the witch's duty to perform rites to obtain these things.

This was probably a matriarchal age, when man was the hunter and woman stayed at home making medicines and magic. As man's intellect and ability to reason developed and he started questioning more his environment, his capacity for undoubted belief in the magic rituals began to wane and with it also diminished their effectiveness. Magic was relegated to a small number of people where it continued its career, sometimes in open hostility with the establishment and seldom tolerated. Probably this is the time when magic started to constitute itself in the Wiccan tradition which is where the word witchcraft comes from. Witchcraft then becomes a religion in its own right.

The Bible tells us of the poor persecuted Witch of Endor, working in secret when all other witches had been driven out of the land.

The ancient and most familiar story of witchcraft is black and fiery — with confrontations between the witches and organized religion, where generally the witch came off worse. The good magic, however, has survived the burnings and the witch hunts through many centuries. This picture depicts the public burning of three witches at Derneburg in 1555.

were driven underground and it is estimated that nine million people were tortured and killed during the persecution in Europe.

An old woman who then lived by herself or who was a nuisance or unpopular was liable to be accused, especially if she kept a pet and talked to it, or talked to herself, as so many lonely old people are apt to do. In England, for example, Matthew Hopkins traveled throughout the country finding those who were unpopular with the Puritan regime and torturing them to produce confessions. A pound a head was paid for all convictions.

But magic also enjoyed periods of unthwarted interest, more often when life was shaky and man needed to relieve his anxiety. He hoped to be able to find reassuring answers in the future and a way to control his adverse fate.

One of these periods was the eighteenth century. Historians call this time the Age of Reason, and yet that same age witnessed the extraordinary outbreak of supposed vampirism in Austria and Hungary, the growth of Scottish high grade masonry and other irrationalist secret societies.

In 1801 Frederick Barret wrote *The Magus*, a book which still today plays an important part in the English revival of magic. There is evidence that he also founded a magic society,

It also tells us of Huldah the Sorceress, living in the state of Jerusalem, who was consulted by the King on high matters of religion which the High Priest could not answer.

Witchcraft had many enemies, yet the greatest one would always be the Church. There were times when the Church left witchcraft undisturbed but when the Papacy became firmly established, the priests treated what they called a satanic cult as a hated rival and tried to persecute it out of existence. The Puritans also took up the work with glee, and between them they almost succeeded in destroying witchcraft forever. This was the infamous time of the Holy Inquisition which, authorized in Spain by Papal Bull in 1478, would not be abolished until as late as 1834. Almost all the witches

Below
Lessons in witchcraft — very often the passing on of magic from one generation to the next happened verbally.

Next page
Pictures of past witchcraft often represented ideas such as this one, where the witch raises a storm, in this case to damage the environment. The powers of good magic, though rest within us and have purpose that is perhaps less dramatic.

In old witches' kitchens the hot cauldron was nothing more than a pot for cooking spells! But with the advent of Macbeth's witches' and their "bubble bubble toil and trouble" it became a reason for uncertain activities and a symbol of black magic. In fact a cooking pot is just as important to good magic for its wholesome and herbal contents.

and there is no doubt that a considerable number of occultists in the nineteenth century in England and the USA based their experiments in ritual magic on what they had learned from his book.

An even stronger influence was then exerted by the writings of Eliphas Levi (1810-1875), a French occultist whose name is still alive today in magic circles.

Our own twentieth century seems to be again one of those times of uncertainty that attracts magic. Technology, politics, space travel and modern medicine find tough competition in astrology, tarot and the arts of witches' covens throughout the USA and Europe. Magazines and other literature abound on the subject of horoscope prediction, divination and black and white magic. Modern magicians even advertise on television!

But today the revival of magic has a meaning that goes way beyond simple relief from tensions and stress. Mankind has reached a point of no-return, where the next step is forcibly discontinuous with the past. It is either total destruction, or complete renewal. We all know about total destruction — a few atom bombs and the job is done.

But complete renewal is more involving. For that we need magic. Man needs to turn around

all the way, inside out like a sock. He needs to go back inside himself to the beginning, the starting point of his forefathers. He needs to find in that place of connection and oneness with existence his freedom of choice — the awareness of his creating essence. That freedom and that awareness is Magic.

Introduction

What is *Good Magic*? First of all I want to clarify that the "magic" expressed in this book is not the same as the "witchcraft" practiced by covens active today all over the world. I do not belong to a coven, nor do I have any firsthand information about the practices of the "old religion". There is a lot of misunderstanding today about witches, witchcraft, magic and so on; people are nervous and worried about these arguments and make one big cauldron of all "esoteric" subjects they happen to be hearing about, and I do not want to add to the confusion.

The ideas presented in this book are my own based on a knowledge transmitted to me by my family. I use some very old concepts and ancient symbols, and part of the information I give is common knowledge in many alternative circles today. This is natural, as all of us draw from that original source of magic which was alive at the beginning of civilization. Drawing the circle, for example, while a concept pertinent to witchcraft, is also found in other times and traditions and is therefore heritage of man rather than of a specific branch of human religion.

Good Magic, such as I portray it, has been practiced by my mother and her mother before her and her mother's mother. (They have involved the men of the family when they would let themselves be involved, which, in those times, was not often.) Their knowledge is part of that patrimony which was once general — and was then forgotten during the course of the centuries. Like many other women they kept that patrimony alive in themselves and by themselves. Maybe they never questioned it, and that's why they did not lose it. Maybe nature just wanted it that way.

The knowledge was transmitted in a natural fashion, as part of everyday life. I doubt that these women ever thought of themselves as being *special* in any way. They just knew that a drink made of a certain combination of herbs would make their jealousies seem less important. They knew it the way we know that aspirin makes a headache go away.

With the last generation came the change. My mother was already aware of knowing things in a different way, and that was confusing to her. I complete this change by realizing and externalizing this knowledge of "magic" as a part of my heritage and of myself, which can help others to find that same heritage in themselves again. I find I am not alone in this. In this century many others must have gone through the same process and are now divulging what they are realizing to be

important hints for self-understanding. *Good Magic* is a new concept, in a way, and a very old one too.

It is old because magic is as old as time. It is new because only recently few people here and there have started seeing the magic experience as something which is the patrimony of all and the right of all, and nothing to do with religion or with supernatural powers or with extraordinary things.

Magic, in this sense, is a "new" rediscovery of man's basic essence, that of the creator. It is the experience of going back to the place inside yourself where nothing has ever happened yet and everything is possible — where you can see yourself creating all of your reality.

This process of rediscovery uses intuition and relaxation, and the help of nature, to bring to the surface the creative patterns already existing. It is not a matter of raising power in order to direct it to a chosen subject, decided a priori to be worthwhile. It is an opening and descending into the roots of your own energy where you will find power, but this power will already be engaged in its true purpose, attributed to it by existence. Then it is not a matter of *doing* something with it, or even of defending oneself from the erracity of it, but simply of following the energy which is unfolding itself. *Good Magic* is not going to tell you how you can change things, but rather how you can discover that which you are and help it grow.

A good magician then is like a good gardener. He knows that changing a rose into another flower is not possible, and that if ever it could be achieved, it would be, at best, just a game. He knows that his job is to sort the weeds from the flowers and to help the flowers grow.

Preparing for Magic

Open the door:
There is magic under the teapot, in your
shoestring...
and in the wind outside, chanting to you.

Magic Requires

TIME

You might feel you simply cannot fit another project into your day. You might think that magic is for gypsies or witches who were born that way anyhow, or that you need to be initiated by some powerful personage — and where are you going to find one, between stretch-aerobic classes, office hours and baby teething problems?

You have picked up this book. Whether you know it or not, magic has already entered your life. Experience magic, even for just a moment, and you will not be the same again. You will see ordinary objects shine like stars — teacups and saucers becoming holy with life; then you will know that whatever you are spending your time on — success, relationship, career, family, money — is only important when it carries inside it that magical quality.

All you need to do at the beginning is to follow the pull of magic. Give yourself a few minutes — maybe before going to sleep, when your children are in bed and you are finished for the day. You don't need to be made-up and dressed — take your most pressing problem and do a little magic for it. See what happens. It will be fun, relaxing and entertaining; something you can do totally alone, something that involves you in an activity that is different, and a pleasure.

You can begin without complications, using a flower or a concoction of herbs or a single candle. The magic circle and the symbols of the elements (see end of this section) are useful, but not a must. In fact nothing in this course of magic is a must, except your willingness and concentration. At first you may not find an extraordinary result from your magic, but you will begin to *feel* what it is to *do* magic. This feeling will stay with you during the rest of the day. You might not notice it, but it will be there, slowly changing and deepening the way you perceive reality.

Maybe one day you will notice that without any special purpose in mind you have bought a bunch of red roses to adorn your bedroom — that same evening you spend a very intense, passionate time with the man or woman in your life. Or you suddenly notice the rhymes of a song going round in your head; you listen to the words and you realize, for example, that there are words in the song that make you aware of something you have been wanting for a long time without being conscious of it. Or you could find yourself replacing the old doormat with a new one — only to greet, later, a long lost friend showing up at your doorstep.

You begin seeing connections, links between experiences which evade your normal casual way of seeing life. You realize more and more the magic connection. You are not doing anything different; you still eat at eight and take the bus to work — but slowly everything finds a new meaning.

Magic rituals and incantations are really only ways of repeating under "laboratory conditions" what is happening in life all the time anyway. Doing them opens your eyes to what you are creating for yourself outside your magic laboratory, in real life, as well as showing you ways in which you can change your life. As you progress in your relationship with magic you see how all of your life's elements are just like pieces of a puzzle which can be moved around by magic, until you form the intended picture — your real self.

Using good magic it is possible to change the normal condition in which we find ourselves running around trying to fulfill ever-growing expectations. Outside factors no longer control us and time can become our own dimension.

Then it is not at all a matter of *finding time*. As you stop running around trying to fulfill ever-growing expectations, outside factors no longer control you, and your time becomes *your* dimension — a magic gift of existence for you to express all that you need to express and create all that you want to create within your own life.

INTENSITY AND CONCENTRATION

Now you want to proceed with exploring the ins and outs of the magic world, but before looking at the moon and gathering herbs, it is necessary to consider just exactly what you have to *be* in order to *do* magic. What do you need to pull out of your own hat, what qualities, what personal attributes? It is not a matter of shining up your past boy-scout memories, or your best achievements as corporate manager. What you need for magic is not so much a quality, as an intention. Everybody is fit for magic, if only they want to be.

In fact *will* is the first requisite of magic. You need to focus on the matter at hand, gather as much emotional steam as you can master and will the thing to happen. Second, and equally important, is your unwavering

Left
Concentration becomes a peaceful awareness of lack of doubt — an art that will become easier and easier and will spill back out into daily life. Buddha, represented opposite, called it meditation.

Next page
The four powers of the Magus are knowledge, courage, will and silence — powers needed to aid your ability to focus and to concentrate on your magic.

belief that what you do is going to succeed. This is not so much a positive action, something you actively do by repeating to yourself, "this is going to work, this is going to work," but more a peaceful awareness of *lack of doubt*. It is not easy to be one hundred percent focused and perfectly calm. It is likely that in your normal day a stressful combination of work and/or family will take you as far from calm and concentration as you can be.

Learning to do magic is like learning to swim — you learn to do it by doing it. Take a little time out each week from your normal occupations and dedicate it to exploring magic; you will find it becomes easier and easier to concentrate totally on the subject you wish to achieve. This ability and the resulting peacefulness will then spill back out into your normal day. Soon you will be able to see your daily activities as acts of magic where life is no longer controlling you, but you are creating it.

THE FOUR POWERS OF THE MAGUS

Knowledge, courage, will and silence: traditionally called the four powers of the magus, these qualities are what you need to aid your ability to focus and to concentrate.

Here are some details:

KNOWLEDGE This is the voice of your inner wisdom, the part in you which *knows*. It is not knowledge in the way you learn at school; it is a knowledge which cannot be acquired for it is to be lived or experienced.

COURAGE When your own, inner truth challenges ideas and preconceptions you have lived with for a long time, you will need courage to follow it.

WILL This is what keeps you on the path, fending off the thousand and one distractions that can take you away from it.

SILENCE This is the ability to shut off the noise of the mind; all the constant thoughts and worries which go around and around in your head. Without this ability, you cannot hear your inner voice.

Nourish these qualities — remember them. You don't need a special setting and a special time to do that. You might be sitting in your office or at the counter of a local store or waiting for the subway... just remember: "Am I listening to myself?"

Remembering the four powers can bring about deep changes in your life. It is in fact the first part of your magic training, and a very important part. Be practical though; don't expect too much too soon. For example, you

might be on a train going to the movies and you remember the four powers. Perhaps you realize that this is not what you really want to do. It is easy to get off the train and go home — in this case you are entirely master of your activities. However, if you are working and your inner voice tells you that this is not the right job for you, it might be a little impractical to get up and leave your job!

Find alternative ways of being, retrain yourself, and explore new possibilities, for magic is about being intelligent, courageous and present. It is an ever-growing process. By remembering the four powers of the magus often, you will enter this process, and while you see your ability to focus and to concentrate grow every day, your life will be changing from mundane to magical.

Preparing Yourself

Having looked at the general requirements of the magic path, let us continue this training by considering what is needed to prepare yourself for a magic ritual.

CLEANSING

When working magic, your mental and emotional spaces are as important as your physical space. Perhaps you cannot at first recognize these parts of yourself as readily, but with a bit of practice you will start seeing them as tangible factors to be kept clean and tidy, to be suited and arranged to your best purpose.

What you are looking for as an ideal inner space for magic is a sense of *unexcited collectedness*. You need to be *present* where you are and with what you are doing, but calm and without expectations. It is possible that finding such space could prove at first a difficult task. Nobody can show you what is right as it changes from person to person, and to begin with, you are likely to be expectant, maybe anxious or even afraid.

Cleansing yourself is therefore of the utmost importance, both in the body and in the mind. Cleansing has been part of religious and magical practices since the beginning of time. It is sufficient to think of the Christian Baptism, where the postulant is immersed in water before receiving the blessing of God.

Through cleansing you wash away all stresses and tensions which you have accumulated in your normal activities. You can think of those tensions as a crust which covers your inner being and hides the true voice. As magic operates from that inner space you see how necessary it is to be cleansed and free to expose yourself.

A CLEANSING METHOD The following is a good general cleansing method that can be used before any magic session.

Run a shower and as you let the cool water (never hot) wash over you, stay still under the jet and feel the contact of the water with your skin. Imagine your emotions: all sadness, anger, frustration, but also excitement, lust, whatever you feel; imagine it to be on the surface of your skin. Using the tables in part two you could also associate colors with it. If you feel angry see the skin of your body covered with the associated color and see the drops of water washing away the color. Remain under the water until the color has all gone. It might take a while; the color might change into a different one — just visualize the water dissolving it, as if your skin was painted with water colors; see the colored water go down the plug. Breathe deep and

Left
Water acts as an inner as well as an outer cleanser and will provide the beginnings of the new order needed to make you pure and ready for the making of good magic.

Below and next page
Clothes touch the skin and the pores breath the cloth constantly so that your choice of materials is most important. Some materials prevent the pores of the skin from breathing freely and this will not enhance your magical work. Linen and silk or other pure materials are best.

steadily into your belly while you are doing this. Let your breath stay normal, though, and don't force it. You are not looking at this moment for any kind of releasing of old emotions but rather for a steady settling of your energy, for a sense of balance. When you feel soft and clear, and relaxed, dry yourself and put on the special clothes which you keep aside for magic.

CLOTHING

Clothes are in direct contact with your skin — your pores breathe them constantly and they are the most direct expansion of your physical state. You should always pay close attention to what you wear — specially when you are performing magic, as those activities heighten your awareness and you would be uncomfortably conscious of anything which might be hindering you.

The material should be natural — such as cotton, wool, or silk. Stay away from man-made fabrics. These do not breathe with you, do not answer to the change in your body temperature and, what is more important, can become barriers to the energy you are trying to free from your body to perform incantations.

I choose plain colors, with no patterns, as I find them less distracting, but that is a matter of personal comfort. Some favor dark colors such as navy blue, black or dark purple while others prefer pure white or other light colors. Traditional witches' covens have their own rules about this, but as we are not here involved with covens, hierarchies and structures, I would advise a small selection of different-colored simple, loose clothes. Every time choose the color which most suits the mood and the need of the day.

CONCENTRATING

Once you are cleansed and clothed, sit comfortably with your eyes shut and closely observe

your mental and emotional space. Look at your thoughts for a few minutes without interfering with the mental process. Notice what your predominant mood is and just let yourself be that way.

Relax your body, specially if you feel any tension anywhere. Follow the flow of your breath without changing it, then gently put aside any feelings or thoughts which might be happening and simply be silent. This may sound a lot easier than it actually is, and you shouldn't worry about just how calm you manage to be. Those who are familiar with meditation will find themselves here on familiar ground, and in truth retracing one's own steps to the clear source of the "Making" is what all religions and teachings, all meditations and techniques are about.

When you reach this calm, collected space you will feel all your emotions, all your thoughts, and all your energies, simply lying there patiently waiting to be summoned. You can then direct them at a target like an archer directs his arrow. It is a readiness and a complete mastery of your own — it starts at a very superficial level, but it deepens every time and with it deepens your magical power. This special power isn't the power of the world, but a more enriching power.

Your Place

THE ROOM

Once you have built your confidence and you know what you are doing and what results you are looking for, you can do magic anywhere.

However, at the beginning of your "learning process", the physical area as well as your mental and emotional space are to be carefully cherished. As we emphasized at the start of this section, concentration is the single most important item which can determine your success and so you must do everything you can to acquire it.

It should be obvious that you cannot easily concentrate on your magic while sitting in a living room full of people and smoke, in front of a TV, munching peanuts and chips.

The best area would be one where you are cut off from your normal activities. It would be ideal, of course, to set aside a room to be used solely for the purpose of making magic. If your bedroom is your own and you don't use it for watching TV or having parties of friends it is a good place to use. But in any case you do need a space where you can be alone for a while every day, a space that you can arrange as you wish — somewhere without disturbance.

Trying to perform magic in a place which is often in use will cause problems and make the magic less successful because the different vibrations from other people will linger in the atmosphere. You would then need to spend a lot of time and energy re-setting the balance in that place.

Your objective is to create an atmosphere of serene concentration. Anything that disturbs you, for whatever reason, has to be removed. If you have a photo of someone close to you on the bedside table, and every time your eyes fall on it you feel a twinge of discomfort, or excitement, you need to remove it. It could be that the emotional situation between you and

Pages 26 and 27
It is, of course, best to have a special room where magic rituals can be conducted — a room where none of the modern diversions such as TV exist to spoil the sense of peace and concentration.

your loved one is heavily charged. Perhaps you feel in your heart that he or she disapproves of your activities.

Look around and consider every object with this in mind. If it is disturbing to your peace, remove it. In the same way, and if you do have the possibility, paint the walls the color most centering for you and lay down a carpet (possibly of a natural fiber) of the same shade. It is best if walls, ceiling and floor are of the same color — that is, of course, if you are using that space only for magic. The continuity of the color will improve your capacity for concentration. A good color for this purpose is usually pale blue, as it is relaxing and soothing.

LIGHTING

It doesn't really matter whether your space is well lit or not; your own sense of serenity is all that counts. Much of the work inside is going to be done in candle light.

ORIENTATION

It is quite important to determine with a compass how your magic place relates to the four cardinal points. During your work you will be either standing or sitting facing east. The east is the direction of sunrise and light; its color is white. Facing east strengthens the power and gives a boost of vitality and freshness.

FURNITURE

Some like to surround themselves with objects and pictures that remind them of magic while others favor simplicity and a spartan environment where only those items that are strictly necessary are permitted. It is a matter of your own preference; just follow your own feelings. Whatever can help you concentrate, whatever can still your mind and make you feel calm and settled, that is what you need.

The two things you will need to have in your magic space are: a place to sit — this can be a comfortable cushion on the floor or a sofa or an armchair, whatever is best for you; and a place to work — a surface on which it is possible to write and to put things. This latter surface can be a simple wooden tablet which you can lay on the floor, if that is what you like. Or it can be a small table, or even the top of a chest. The important thing is that you take great care with your surface: you need to put it away safely every time, if you use it only for magic. If at other times you use it for other activities, you

A protector is invested with the property to charge the atmosphere of a place which will otherwise be in common use. The protector can be kept safely out of the way and will retain its powers. The protector can be anything that reminds you of the magic you do.

need to make sure to thoroughly cleanse it before magic, re-consecrating it every time.

The above arrangements are, of course, ideal. It may not always be possible in every individual situation to accomplish the luxury of a perfect, private place for magic. Life is busy, space is limited and people often overwhelm our time and space. This does not mean, however, that making your magic is impossible. It may mean that you need to make a greater effort to get started but very often this increased energy can actually have a beneficial result — so don't despair. Take note of the following additional possibilities to aid you in arranging your surroundings for magic work.

THE PROTECTOR

If your space is such that necessarily it has to be used other than by yourself it is advisable to have an object, such as a statue, or a crystal, or a framed image, which we can call your *protector*. You can invest it with the property to *charge* the atmosphere and as you will be able to put it away safely when you are not using it for magic, it will not be corrupted by other people and situations.

The protector can be anything that reminds you of the magic. It might be an effigy of a buddha or of an ancient god or goddess. It can be an abstract futuristic image or something you have yourself carved in wood or stone. If you do not already have something which feels right, take your time and look for it. There will be no mistake when you really find it because you will know that it is what you want. You will know because in your mind there will not be even a shadow of doubt when you have found it. Most important is to drop all preconceptions of what the object should be.

Of course even if you do have a permanent magic space, you can still own a protector which can stay there undisturbed. In fact, I know quite a few people who, without even knowing what it is, have such a protector and carry it with them wherever they might move, knowing only that they particularly like it and that they feel something special when looking at it.

Magic Places in Nature

You have seen how to set up and prepare your own magic space indoors, but naturally the world has a lot more to offer than a small room. When there is time enough and the weather permits it, there is nothing better than going to a silent, secluded place in nature. There you can directly connect with the elements and feel readily under your finger-tips the energies of existence as you caress the trees, touch the flowers, and listen to the sounds of nature.

Nature provides often the most private and magical places for magic — all that is needed is that you can be alone in your chosen place and that the place you choose agrees with you.

The only two requisites should be that you can be alone in your chosen spot and that this spot agrees with you. You might have to organize a special trip for this purpose, perhaps several days long, but it will be worth it. Everyone needs some kind of contact with nature to feel balanced and grounded, and that is so much more true for those who are learning to use nature's forces for magic. The second requirement: to find a spot that actually agrees with you. This might need some research work and a little intuition. What does it mean: "a spot that agrees with you"? It is a place in nature which makes you feel good. You might equally like the seaside and the mountains, but if you go to the sea after a while you become tired and sluggish and in the end maybe even depressed. If you go to the mountains, on the other hand, it might be hard work walking up the steep hills, but you feel refreshed, alive and awake. You must be aware of exactly what it is that makes you feel a particular way when surrounded by a particular aspect of nature and of all your feelings, not just those that appreciate the beauty of nature.

Here is a list of power aspects of nature for you to check out before you make your final decision: seaside; mountain tops; waterfalls; lakeside; rivers, streams, brooks; caves and large rocks; wide, flat fields; woods. If you have a busy and hectic life that keeps you occupied the whole week, you can make this into a program of several weekends. You could go alone or with your family or friends, taking a notebook with you to write down faithfully your reactions to that place. Having this task of finding your magical spot in nature will be a good excuse to go out of town, putting you in an explorer frame of mind, which can make

into fun something that otherwise you might not bother doing. You can organize trips of a few hours, of a day or a weekend — or if you wish, do your entire research in one go of several days.

It will be especially good if you have already read through the whole book and can prepare an incantation to do in the spot you have chosen. This will give you a final proof of the suitability of that place.

Regardless of where you are you need to remember to define your place. Take a compass with you and determine the east, west, north and south. At a few steps distance from each other mark those points with a vase or a candle or an oil lamp. This will help you to contain the energies that you will raise with the magic. As a general rule you will be sitting facing east. (Unless you are performing a sunset ceremony, in which case you would be facing west.)

Tools of Magic

PRIMARY TOOLS

A primary tool for magic is any being or object of nature which is used in a magical practice by channeling its own and particular properties into the goal you want to achieve. All things of nature are magical — as there is life in them, so there is magic. One flower possesses healing qualities, another one the faculty of opening your sight into the future. Yet unless these properties are used, the flower will just grow, bloom and die. The same is true for each tree, rock, seashell, little fish or bird or lion of nature.

To discover nature in this light of magic and to use her gifts as primary tools for magic is the most enriching experience man can make. Once you see the world made up of this vibrating magic which you are part of, you are no longer

A primary tool can be any being or object in nature which can be used for channeling its own particular properties into the magical goal you have in mind. Because everything in nature is alive it is also magical, carrying powers and healing qualities that are inherent to each individual thing.

alone — everything is your companion in the process of creation.

How does it happen? How do you pick up a seashell or a plant and become able to use it for magic? You do it by opening yourself totally to the particular being you want to do magic with. Take the seashell in your hands and look at it; feel it with your fingers, feel it with your heart, smell it, and open your spirit to whatever her spirit is, without words in your head, without knowledge and history. You will be unable to do this if, as soon as you see a shell, your mind is already running through the biological, oceanalogical, chemical, and mythological files on it. The experience must be totally new. Don't expect a lot at the beginning... and trust what you feel. When you are far advanced in the path of magic, and you can see all things with naked eyes, every single particle in nature is available to you in that way.

But to begin with it is a long process of acquaintance, of opening and loving. It takes time and patience. You will need to get to know your friends slowly and to find what is the best way to relate to them, what are the areas they can best help you with. You will need to find out if there are some days when these friends can help you better, and under what conditions.

It is a real love affair which you are to begin

with your chosen subject, and as such you need to have the greatest respect and care for your primary tools. Do not be deceived by the word used here: tool. It does not mean that you are to treat your subject as a thing even though it might be a stone or a seashell; it just means that you will use and channel the magic contained in it.

People can also be primary tools of magic. It is sufficient to think of a love affair with another person; when the love is strong you live magical moments with that person. You are, maybe without knowing it, using that person as a channel to the realm of the magic world.

Within magic there are many ordinary tools needed to help the magic happen, mostly for practical reasons. With these items you will have a relationship with utility.

When you know how, you can expand those moments, and you can channel that great energy to make discoveries and achieve impossible feats.

This pre-supposes a great clarity of mind and of heart, sound wisdom, and openness of spirit. People working magic with each other in this way need to be either under the guidance of a teacher or very advanced souls. As it is a very complex theme, it transcends the scope of this book.

As an introduction to nature's magical primary tools, Herbs, Flowers and Stones are presented in part two of this book. They were chosen because they are easy to work with and with some precaution are quite safe for anybody to use. Furthermore they are channels which can help you in a wide range of needs in the magical practice.

You can begin with them, if you want to. Or start off with another tool that appeals to you more. Either way remember that patience and respect are needed in discovering the ways of releasing and channeling magic in the aspects of nature.

ORDINARY TOOLS

These are all those man-made objects which you will need in the course of your operations. With them you have a relationship of utility, and though these things are also made from natural substances and contain magic, you are only using them in that dimension.

A magician has quite a few of those tools, depending on what kind of magic he favors. If he likes to work with herbs, for example, he will have many gardening tools as ordinary magic tools. If he likes to work with birds, he will need all the paraphernalia used for keeping birds. The important thing is to remember

never to use your ordinary magic tools for
anything else than for magic.

Here is a list of the most needed ordinary
tools:

THE CAULDRON The traditional magic
tool. This can be a fire-proof terra-cotta or cast
iron pot. It is used to boil herbs and other
concoctions.

OIL LAMP AND CANDLES These are most
important because they are the only form of
illumination possible when the sunlight or
moonlight are not enough. Electric light is, in
fact, as bad for magic as garlic is for ghosts.

NOTEBOOK AND PEN Choose a cloth-
bound book, not leather, and use it to record
your experiments, your spells, your magical
dates. The pen should be a simple goose-feather
quill, but if you find it too difficult to write
with that, choose a good fountain pen — not a
biro or felt-tip! — and use it *only* for magic.

A MIRROR This is essential as mirror-
magic is very effective and easy. It does not
have to be a big one, but when not used for
magic it must be covered with a cloth of black
velvet. If you want to avoid embarrassing
questions it is better not to use a wall mirror for
this purpose!

THE CUP, THE INCENSE HOLDER, THE
BRASS BOWL, THE BURNER These serve to

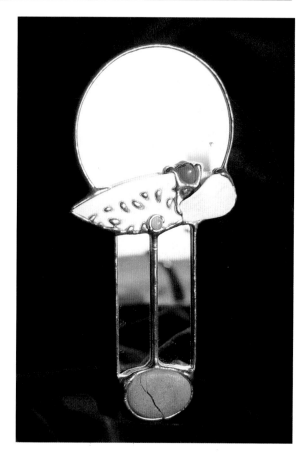

represent the four elements in the magic circle,
and you also always need them in front of you
in the opening ceremony.

The cup (representing water) serves to contain water or wine and should be silver or

Left
The burner, the cup, the brass bowl and the incense holder — each serving to represent the elements within the magic circle and for constant use in the opening magic ceremony.

Below
No good magician can do without the broom, even if only to show to those inquiring friends!

ceramic. The incense holder (incense representing air) can be a ready-made one (brass or wood) for incense sticks, or if you know incenses well could be a proper censer or a thurible. In this book I don't treat the subject of incenses in detail, as it would take up too much space — nevertheless incense is one of the most beautiful ways of doing magic. The brass bowl (representing earth) — could also be ceramic — serves to contain rice or other grains. The burner (representing fire) is a cast iron little pot or similar object that serves to light a small wood fire.

The above objects can naturally be used also in any rituals or incantations in which they might be needed. If, for example, you need to drink a potion, the cup can be used; if you want to burn a herb, use the burner, and so on.

THE BROOM Just can't do without it! Choose an old garden one, and show it to your friends when they inquire about your magical activities.

Times

We should now consider one important element in the practice of magic: timing. Are some times better than others? How to tell?

In the first place you need to take care of your immediate needs and obligations. It will not do at all to chant incantations when you are supposed to be in your office, or the children are screaming and the washing needs doing: if you can arrange to be free only on Friday nights and Monday mornings, then it is better to use those times to their best advantage, regardless of other considerations. It is better to dedicate only an hour a week to magic, and be serene, than to greet the day with a full morning ceremony every day...and miss the bus.

However, if you can keep track of certain timing factors, your magic will benefit greatly from it. There are many such factors, but the three most important ones are: the different energy of the day and of the night and the times when day and night meet; the phases of the moon; and the winds.

DAY AND NIGHT

During the day the energy of the sun is predominant. It is strong, active and expanding. Sunshine "draws you out"; it makes you want to explore and try new things, it gives you courage, helps communication, business and commerce. It is the Yang (male) of the Chinese philosophy.

During the night the moon is queen. Her energy is cool and soft, receptive, introspective and mysterious. It furthers meditation and silence, poetry and art. It is the Yin (female) of the Chinese philosophy.

Daytime furthers all magic which involves relating to others, expanding in the world, gaining strength and power. Work and money are dealt with best during the day, so are matters of travel and those stages of a love affair where building and expanding are required.

While prosperity is a daytime magic, fertility is for the night, because of its essentially receptive quality. Rituals aimed at discovering some hidden truth within ourselves should happen in the night, and so should attempts at communicating from inside with someone far away. Divination magic is usually performed during these hours as is astral projection and other esoteric experiences.

SUNRISE AND SUNSET

But it is specially when night and day meet, at sunrise and sunset, that miracles can happen; it

Pages 46 and 47
Sunrise and sunset are as important in the arts of magic as the phases of the moon. It is at these times that the body, the mind and the spirit are at their most energetic and vulnerable so that magical work can function best.

Pages 48 and 49
The four phases of the moon, waxing, waning, full and black, are of the greatest importance to all those involved in magic. The power of the moon to pull or relax through her natural gravitational and magical strength will decide, very often, whether or not your own magic is going to succeed.

is those times which you must treasure for magic.

If you have not done it before, stay awake once all night and watch the darkness slowly open to reveal misty forms and colors, and then watch how, suddenly, the first rays of sun break through and burst everything into subtle life. You cannot fail to notice the magical quality of these moments. Be prepared to work your magic and then you will be able to channel and use the energy released by the waking earth.

You must be ready though! You will only get a cold if you are nodding off, half frozen in front of an open window at four a.m! Set your alarm well before sunrise and prepare yourself carefully. Your sacrifices will surely be rewarded. (An example of a morning ritual is in part three).

All kinds of magic can benefit greatly by being performed in the sunrise hour, and especially this is the time for incantations regarding new beginnings: for finding a new love, a new job or even a new direction in life. To regain hope and trust in the future after having suffered a bad time, to regain health after an illness and to heal a broken heart. For sunrise, as for sunset magic, it is good to be outside or in someway in contact with nature

— sitting on your patio or balcony or in front of an open window. Remember always to be facing east, for the east sees the rising of the sun.

Sunset is an equally magical time. It is not unusual to feel a sudden and poignant sadness at this time of day — as the light fades into darkness, the day is gone. If you are in a receptive mood, every sunset can be like a small death. The moment to render your accounts and become aware of how you have spent your energies. With the advent of electricity sunset has certainly lost most of its impact — with the lights on and the television blasting, the sun will set totally unobserved unless you make a point to watch the sunset.

Yet it is a very important time, one of the best moments to know about oneself, and specially in times of confusion and stress it is fruitful to use it as such — in this context sunset magic is very productive. Whenever you want to know the truth about something, use the power of the last rays of the sun as they linger in the horizon. Whether it is a truth someone is keeping from you or that you are keeping from yourself, if you channel the energy of the creatures of nature as they prepare for the night you will not fail to receive an answer to your questions. Remember to face

west, the point of the setting sun, for magic in this time.

MIDDAY AND MIDNIGHT

When the sun is at its highest in the sky is the time to use its power in full. Use it for vigor, strength, health and to give an extra burst of energy to any kind of magic.

The darkest hour, midnight, is for banishing magic. If there is anything you want to get rid of — an attitude, a habit, an idea, something which you wish to be gone from your life — midnight is the time to do it. (Mind, I am not talking about your awkward neighbor!) If then you choose a night of waning moon when a north wind is blowing, you cannot fail. (See below about times of the moon and winds.)

THE PHASES OF THE MOON

It is a well-known fact that the influence of the moon is a very important element in the fluctuations of the psychic energy. With the same power that she uses to raise the tides of the sea the moon plays upon humans' souls, specially of women, who since the beginning of time have learned to recognize the ways and powers of the moon and how to use them.

WAXING MOON   The moon is called waxing when she goes from black to full. As the moon grows she will exercise a magnetic pull on all things exposed to her energy. It is the perfect time for a fertility magic or for the magic to protect the beginning of a love affair, to increase health and well-being, to set off on new avenues of the spirit. It is also a good time to plant magic herbs and to begin incantations which have a longer time spell to be completed.

WANING MOON   From full to black, the moon is called waning. This is a time for undoing, for receding, for eliminating and separating. If you wish a peaceful ending to a love affair or a business partnership this is the moment to operate on it. It is the time to let go of past experiences or of an undesired part of yourself. In the best witches' tradition it is the time to remove warts or, more up-to-date, to

start a weight-loss magic program (see part three). Old times witches were said to put curses on people during this phase of the moon, which were called, precisely, "wanions". The waning moon is also the best time to cut herbs and flowers (see part two).

FULL MOON   The full moon is the high tide of psychic powers and can be helpful in all types of magic. When a specially important or difficult task is at hand use the great power of the full moon.

For some people the time of the full moon is a difficult one: they become edgy and ill-at-ease. While I would discourage such people from attempting a full moon magic right away (healing or otherwise), I would advise them not to try escaping the strong influence the moon is exercising on them. These people should use the waning moon for a magic to help themselves cool out their responses to the full moon, and relax in times of full moon, pursuing possibly a creative and fun activity. (See the magic called "Making Friends with the Full Moon" in part three.)

BLACK MOON   Finally we come to the nights of black moon, or no moon. I find these times should be respected as the magician's Sundays — a rest period, where it is best not to attempt any magic at all.

THE WINDS

The third important element to be considered is the wind. If we were captains of a sail boat we would well understand the importance of knowing and harnessing the forces of the winds. In a way, in magical terms, that is what we are doing: directing the boat of our energy amongst the forces of the known and unknown powers around us. Winds can be as useful to us as they are to that captain in the middle of the sea. According to the direction they blow from, we can recognize four basic types of wind:

THE NORTH WIND   It is cold and dry, his element is earth and the color black. It is a wind of death, intended in its spiritual sense of abandoning those issues which no longer serve us. Therefore, like the time of midnight and the

Pages 50, 51 and below
The wind represents our power to direct the boat of our energy as it floats out amidst the known and unknown forces of the worlds around us. The windsock, a simple device which you can either make or buy, will tell you the directions of the wind — much needed when deciding the incantations, feelings and approaches to magic.

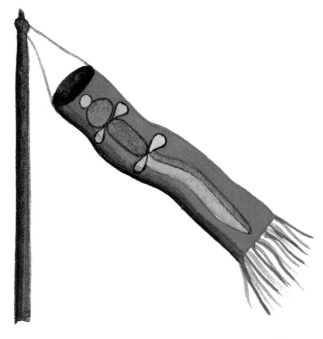

waning moon, north wind provides a good environment for banishing, decreasing and eliminating magic. Because of his correspondence with the element earth (see "The Four Elements") it is also helpful in magic concerning practical matters, the household, the material side of carrying out duties, etc.

THE WEST WIND   It is moist and fertile. Its element is water and the color blue. It is a gentle, soothing wind, which eases aches and pains both physically and emotionally. It is good to use it therefore as a background to healing magic, cleansing and fertility magic. Needless to say, all love magic cannot but be helped by this soft presence.

THE SOUTH WIND   It is hot and dry and very powerful. Its element is fire and its color red. It can help any kind of magic to which it will give an added boost of strength. When fear is the problem, the south wind with his fiery presence can be a real boost — in the warmth it creates, fear loses his cold grip and soon enough even the coldest of hearts is melting.

THE EAST WIND   It comes from Oriental lands of light. It is a cold, dry, bracing wind. Its color is white and the corresponding element is air. It is fresh and stimulating and clears the mind. It is a wind for new starts, improvements and changes. All matters related to the intellect

can be helped by an east wind. It also helps travel and communication.

Combining together these elements can be difficult, but if you do it, you can achieve an extremely powerful background to your practices. For example, you are preparing a magic to aid a new love which needs gentle boosting. You will have a perfect environment if you could choose for your magic a time when: the moon is waxing; a west wind is blowing; it is at sunrise.

DAY		Expanding.
NIGHT		Inverting.
SUNRISE		New beginnings.
SUNSET		Truth finding.
MIDDAY		Extra power.
MIDNIGHT		Banishing.
WAXING MOON		Growth.
WANING MOON		Letting go of things.
FULL MOON		Extra power.
BLACK MOON		Do not do magic.
NORTH WIND		Finishing, closing, separating, getting out.
EAST WIND		Changes, new beginnings, intellect, communication.
SOUTH WIND		Fire, passion, initiative, strength.
WEST WIND		Cleansing, purifying, love, gentleness.

Examples:

NEW LOVE   BANISH JEALOUSY   IMPROVE WORK CONDITIONS

These symbols appear in each incantation of part three for quick reference.

Elements of Magic

THE FOUR ELEMENTS

We come now to the study of a very important subject in this course of magic: the magic of the four elements. So far you have seen how to prepare yourself and your place, how to choose a time when the right forces for your magic are acting; you know what magic tools are and which you need. What you need now is the background, the soil in which magic can concretize.

Magic is made in the mind — it is first and foremost an act of the will — but to materialize this will, to make it happen concretely in the world, the four elements are needed: air, fire, water and earth. They are the ground, the material magic uses to spin her cloth. Without the elements, magic would remain in the land of dreams. It is necessary, therefore, to get acquainted with them and their ways and what they represent.

Of course we all know that air is light and you breath it in and out, fire is hot and burns, water is wet and quenches your thirst, earth is solid, dark and moist. Most of you are perhaps also well aware of the correspondences of the elements in the inner world: air represents the world of thoughts, images and their expression; fire initiative, passion and intuition; water

Air is represented by birds on the wing — freedom and space — light and ever expanding — immeasurable and never contained.

emotions, feelings and sensitivity; earth structure, consistency and physical things.

Magic serves herself using the elements, inside and outside, to make your wishes come true. If you need a better job you will need the air of communication and connections necessary to get you where you want to be, the fire of initiative, the water of emotions to know the direction your heart wishes you to take, and the earthiness of the material conditions. How you contact these forces is explained in the end of this section under the heading "Calling the Powers". But for now it is important to consider each of the elements, and how magic can be expressed through them.

AIR

Air is the element of the birds on their wings... the element of freedom and spaciousness. Air is light and expanding, therefore difficult to be measured and contained. It represents the world of thoughts, and it is often said of someone who is very thoughtful that he has "his head in the clouds". The ability to reason and synthesize is what raises man above pains and pleasures as it shows him what part these experiences have in the whole process and makes them acceptable. Through air you can

have an idea of the direction you want your life to take, and when fire combines with it, there is nothing that can stop you. But a poor air functioning will see you stranded in your own particular world without the breath of vision to carry yourself ahead.

AIR MAGIC

WORDS   Words in magic can be put together to form spells, or they can be used alone as ways of channeling power. Making spells is an essential art in magic, as spells are used in most forms of rituals and incantations. Although it is possible to do magic without uttering a single word, it is very difficult.

You do not need a gift with words to be able to create spells, as it is based on the repetition of a few sentences which make sense to you — and not necessarily to anybody else. At the beginning of part three you can find an extensive introduction in the art of creating your own spells. Words alone, repeated with intensity and concentration have magical powers too. To discover which word is magical for you, you must try by repeating to yourself words that have a resonance in your own being. The word could be, for example: abundance; this word, repeated to yourself with the due force, would

release in you the desired forces, it would be your *word of power*. No one can tell you which your word of power can be. It probably will also change in the course of your life, as your direction changes. The word of power is used like the protector which you have already read about. It instantly creates a condition inside yourself of concentrated strength and awareness through which magic is possible. It can be used anywhere, and it does not have to be pronounced aloud. It can also be used in moments of stress or when feeling low. Be careful, though, not to overdo it. Repeating your word of power incessantly, or worse,

telling it to anybody who wishes to know it, would deplete it completely.

VISUALIZATIONS This is a very good way to make desired events happen. For visualization magic it is important to choose a time where all the right forces are acting — the right moon phase, the right winds, etc. — and it is also important to prepare yourself very carefully — purifying, clothing, concentrating. During visualization magic it is also important to have some other method happening at the same time, for example, having a candle burning or drinking the right infusion. That is because visualizations are very unstable and need to be *fixed*

Fire makes passion, enthusiasm and desire — both
heat and light...fire brought man from animal to
human.

with outside elements. They are however extremely powerful when you can *stay* in one.
Visualizing a happy event properly does un-
failingly bring it to pass.

MIRROR MAGIC This method also belongs
to air magic since it has to do with images and
memories. It can be used in two ways: to
overcome some inner problem by talking to
your image in the mirror and to "see" into the
past and the future.

The correspondence of the air element is east
and the color white. It can be represented by
the smoke of the incense. Some use a knife to
represent the element air.

Fire and air move upwards; expanding,
moving elements — they are the two aspects of
the Yang of creation of the Chinese philosophy.
Water and earth move downwards; resilient,
passive elements — they are the aspects of the
Yin of creation, the female within the balance
of nature.

FIRE

"Fire embodies passion, enthusiasm and desire.
It is both heat and light...". The harnessing of
fire is the one act in the history of man which
marks his change from animal to human; it
represents both the light of intelligence and the

courage to follow it. It is the spark of passion
and initiative.

Fire shares with water some kind of intrinsic
quality of life: fire makes things warm, water
lush and full, and together they make them
alive. Just as in the case of low water functioning, low fire functioning does not impair a
person's basic ability to survive, but it dras-
tically impairs the capability to enjoy life.
Excessive fire is dangerous as fire destroys
everything in its wake, but poor fire is just as
unhappy: a poor fire person is cold, slow to act
or passive, without enthusiasm for his life and
himself. Fire magic will help to regain the spark
of initiative, bring courage and passion, help to
destroy the old and go ahead with the new.

FIRE MAGIC

BONFIRE MAGIC This can be performed outside, building a bonfire in a chosen spot of
nature, or inside, lighting the fire in the burner
or fireplace. Whether you are inside or outside
this type of fire magic lends itself well to being
performed inside the circle.

Bonfire magic usually involves burning something: either a herb or a flower or a piece of
paper on which you have written some words.
The things you are burning represent that

which you want to be rid of — in fact bonfire magic is an excellent banishing method. For some people it is possible to see sights of future events in the flickering flames.

CANDLE MAGIC This is another easy, useful method. It can be practiced anywhere, anytime. It requires the minimum amount of preparation and time. In fact (if you don't mind people's curiosity) you can even have a candle burning for your magical purpose in the office or in the kitchen. You can always say that it is a smoke-eating candle, or mosquito repelling!

The candles are usually chosen of the color required for your magic, and they are left to burn — after you have pronounced the right words. Sometimes a candle has to burn for three days and three nights, which means replacing it as soon as it is too low. When used together with flowers, candle magic can be a beautiful and soft way to deal with delicate problems: love issues, creativity efforts, friends. Candle magic, anyway, lends itself to any kind of purpose when used in conjunction with the appropriate tools.

SUN MAGIC Magic related to our beautiful star must be considered as fire magic. It is the best way to help new beginnings in work and career matters, but also in love and health. Ways of channeling the light of the sun for magic are explained in part three.

Fire's correspondence is south and the color red. It can be represented by a lighted burner. (As candles are already used in the circle to find the cardinal points.)

WATER

Water flows from the inside of rocks or pours gently from above, like feelings which "well up" inside you or sweep over you. Tears, water

Wells have always had that feeling of age — and well magic is one of the most ancient. Using well magic, provided the water is uncontaminated, will always insure success. Well water can be used close to or away from the well, even at home, but bear in mind that fresh water goes stale within a very short time — sometimes even within a few hours.

flowing from the eyes, are the outward expression of a strong emotional content. Indeed, feelings are made of the same stuff as water: they can be felt cool and refreshing on the skin — but try to grab them, try to get hold of them, they elude you and pool only where they find a gentle place to rest. Water imbibes all life forms and gives them lushness and freshness. Without any feelings the soul would not be a soul at all, but an arid desert of calculations and speculations based upon reactions on the physical surroundings.

Poor water functioning causes a person to be arid, distant, cold and unresponsive. On the other hand excessive water is like a river which exceeds its banks and can wipe away all sense of reality and measure. In cases of poor water functioning water magic is very helpful. But be careful not to use water magic in the case of excessive water functioning. As for all the other elements you must remember not to deal directly with excesses but to find out which element is lacking. Nourishing that one the balance will be automatically redressed without danger.

WATER MAGIC

SEASIDE MAGIC   This includes all incantations and rituals which happen by and use the forces of the sea, the sand, the shells... It usually involves a trip to the seaside. Seaside magic is appropriate for love matters, as the sea energy is deep and soft, but also strong and changeable — like love. If, moreover, the sea is one of your favorite magic spots in nature (see heading "Magic Places in Nature") you can be sure to be able to use the seaside for your magical practices to a good profit.

If a trip to the seaside is not possible, use seashells and other seaside items like dried starfish, stones, sand. Lay them in front of you in your magical place and visualize the sea. That can be enough.

WELL MAGIC   This is a very ancient tradition in magic. Wells have always been associated with magical practices and indeed to use the water of a well for a water magic incantation will assure success. It might not be very easy to find a well — specially if you live in a town or a built up area. I am afraid there are no short-cuts to this one. For well magic, you will have to find a well. However, it is possible, for example, to take the well water home and perform the magic there. Or if you are using a stone you can expose it to the magic of the well during the day, and then, once you are back home, in the night hours pronounce your

Rituals can often involve burying items in offering to
the powers of the earth. The right time, place and
environment will decide the success of the magic and
these factors have to be considered in the light of
your magical knowledge.

incantation. In fact, well magic is a magic which is performed in the night, and always when the moon is waxing or full — never waning. It is a very powerful and deep magic that can release insights into the most hidden truths of your being — and not only yours. If you need to know what someone thinks, how that person is doing, what he or she is doing, well magic is what you need.

Naturally you must always make sure of your intents. If you want to know about the health of another person, or how and where they are out of love, the magic can help you. If you are trying to manipulate somebody out of your own fears or even worse, anger, all you will see in the magic mirror of the well water is a reflection of these (can be frightening, I would not try).

Well magic can involve drinking the water of the well (if it is fresh and pure); the water can also be used in conjunction with herbs to make infusions and magical potions. Another method, as above, is to dip your chosen stone in the well and leave it there for a short period, then take the stone home and let it release the power.

In part three there are examples of well magic. To create new rituals involving wells it is good to follow the examples a couple of times...

then to ask your intuition to release new ways.

BATHROOM RITUALS This very domestic form of water magic is nevertheless very effective. They are appropriate for health and beauty incantations.

Water's correspondent point in the circle is west, its color blue. A cup is usually used, with some liquid inside which can be water or wine, to represent it.

EARTH

Earth is the ground we step on, it is the home and mother, it is the source and provider for all physical needs. The element earth in the inner world represents sensations. Feeling good or bad, feeling sensuous or isolated, being at ease or uncomfortable. It represents where you come from — the animal instincts, which guide you surely to food and shelter, to warmth and security.

An "earthy" person is one who has his feet firmly on the ground, who does not dream much and moves well in the clearly defined realms of physical living — the kitchen, the fields, the work — providing steadily for tomorrow. Without this basic function a person is like a leaf in the wind — unable to attach himself to any identifiable reality and to draw

nourishment and security from it. Where the earthy functions are impaired or confused there prevails a sense of insecurity, of loss and of aloneness.

EARTH MAGIC

BURYING   These are rituals involving burying things and making offerings to the earth. Taking a stone (the appropriate one) and burying it under a certain tree at the right time is earth magic. Or it could be preparing a special bread and offering it to your special spot in nature, where ants and squirrels and other animals will feed from it. This method works well for issues of work and money.

ISOLATING ONESELF IN NATURE   This is another very powerful aspect of earth magic. To be done *only* when the meteorological conditions are favorable and when one is experienced about surviving alone in the wild.

It can release a strong power, and it is specially good for purification rituals and to ask for extra strength and vigor.

PERFORMING ROUTINE ACTIONS IN A SPE-CIAL WAY   This magic is effective and has the advantage of not needing to take any time out of your usual activities. In fact you are still doing the same things, for example cooking or typing or driving your car, but through a specific inner preparation and knowledge you are transforming these actions into magical rituals. This is a good method for invoking clarity. If you are confused about something and need to find your roots, your basic stand, this method is right.

The correspondence of earth in the circle is north and its color black. It can be represented by a handful of rice or other grain in a brass or terra-cotta bowl. Some, instead, use a stone to represent it, others a pentacle. Choose the symbol you are most comfortable with.

The Magic Circle

CASTING THE CIRCLE

Many aspiring witches are aware of the need to paint a circle around them on the ground when doing magic rituals — in fact the use of a circle to mark a sacred area goes back in time as far as we can see. Stonehenge is just one example of the circle used for spiritual/magical purposes in ancient times. To be able to cast a circle is indeed a prerequisite to any successful magic — though here we are not just talking of the round shape drawn on the ground but also and especially of the circle of energy called the aura, which surrounds and envelops our physical body. This circle, which some people can see quite clearly with their naked eyes, is always there as long as there is life in the body — when we are balanced and healthy it is unbroken and compact and it looks somehow like an egg made of strings which all start from the top of our head and go round to the soles of our feet. If we are ill, tense, worried, angry or in any way disturbed this will show in the pattern of these lines. They become slack and limp and show gaps in their color vibrations. When we are well and balanced and at peace the lines are supple and tight and are easily perceived by their color vibrations. By concentrating and visualizing your energy lines you can adjust their shape and color till they are in perfect harmony and beautiful shape. Sitting inside the circle which you have drawn on the ground you see your aura, the complete circle of energy which surrounds and supplies you like electricity supplies a light bulb. You are a complete circuit in yourself and need nothing else — you are whole and complete.

Casting the circle then is both an external and an internal exercise. In fact, as often is the case, doing it externally by marking a circle on the floor around the place where you want to work will help you do it internally. As the recalling of the inner circle of energies serves the purpose of making you stronger and harmonized, so the drawing of the circle on the ground will help you concentrate your powers. Some believe the circle is drawn to keep evil influences at bay. Never think in those terms — as existence mirrors your beliefs, if you feel the need to keep demons at bay, she will provide you with the raw material. The circle is used to contain energy, and it is meant to be a mirror, an outside manifestation of the energy body, or aura, that surrounds the physical body.

The outer circle can be drawn on the floor with white chalk using a piece of rope two and one-half meters long so that the diameter of the

Pages 66 and 67

The simplest method of making your magic circle is first to take a piece of string which should be the length of half the circle you want to draw (bearing in mind that you will have to sit in it afterwards) — up to seven meters across. Next, having drawn the line, take a piece of paper and fold it into a flute. Fill the flute with flour and allow the flour to pour out along the line of the circle until complete. Next take a compass and find out where the north lies on the circle — mark it by placing your candles and seat yourself inside.

circumference will be five meters. If you are working outside or there is more than one person, it can be up to nine meters in diameter. If your space is smaller just adapt the circle to whatever space you can manage. The circle should always be drawn clockwise, or deosil, and it is good to determine the four cardinal points on it: east, south, west and north, and to mark them with four white candles, one at each point. You can use more candles for extra illumination but be careful to place them outside the circle. You should then be sitting inside your circle facing east, as I have mentioned earlier in this section.

The four elements also need to be represented in the circle, and you have seen what to use to represent them in the previous heading "The Four Elements".

This is a table of the elements and their correspondence both within ourselves and in space:

AIR	East	Thoughts	Incense	Expression
FIRE	South	Intuition	Burner	Initiative
WATER	West	Emotions	Cup	Depth
EARTH	North	Sensation	Rice bowl	Security

As you find your space and complete yourself, face in turn the four candles representing the four cardinal points of the circle. Look at the object representing the connected element and let the life of that element fill you up.

For example, starting with the air face the incense holder and silently watch the smoke of incense rising in the element air. As you imagine you are made of air, you will feel yourself weightlessly floating in the atmosphere. Leave behind all cares and ties and be free. Face the south candle and look at the flame of the burner, then close your eyes and let the element fire fill you up completely. See your body as if it were made of flames. Hear its rumbling, crackling sounds, imagine the fire burning, incinerating your personality, your identity, until you are no more than a dancing flame. Face west and the cup holding the element water. See your body made of gentle rippling waves, feel its fluidity and coolness. Melt into the water element all extremes of passions, all fears, anxieties, pains and pleasures until it is all united in a single oceanic wave of energy.

Finally come to rest at the fourth gate of your circle, north and earth. Let the moist dark earth welcome you in its womb, dissolve your physical boundaries and die in it.

Redressing the balance. If you lack the element of "air" — representing thoughts and words and numbers — a computer, played with just for fun, is good to bring this element higher in you. If you lack fire, take someone's hand in yours and feel the warmth, and if earth is your missing element, bring your hands and thoughts to the earth by gardening or if there is no garden, simply planting indoor pots or window boxes.

REDRESSING THE BALANCE

Very likely one of the elements will attract you more than the others; at the same time another one will feel uncomfortable to you. The reason is that hardly anybody is in perfect balance, and it is normal to have a little too much energy of one element and too little of the other. Feeling the various elements inside yourself, while you surround yourself physically by their symbols and the circle drawn on the floor, serves the purpose of re-establishing the balance between them. The elements will act like the poles of an electrical circuit and will make the energy field surrounding you stronger and healthier, giving you both increased well-being and increased awareness of all your faculties.

Casting the circle is in itself an ever growing process and the first and most important magical practice. It is good to give it the utmost care and to try to bring the elements within yourself in balance. You can have a lot of fun with it. You will notice that the elements work in couples, or axes of energy. For example your air-fire axis might be out of synchronization, pulling too much or too little on one pole. Focus on the element that is weaker rather than on the one that is stronger, and set yourself to reinforce it. Visualize the energy axis and see it

The element of water moves through your body, slows you down. It is an inner spring belonging to the world of emotions and there is no forcing it, only allowing it to flow.

freeing itself; see the current flowing unhindered from one pole to the other. Tune in to the element you are missing and ask it, as if it were a friend, what you can practically do to strengthen it. Relaxing and tuning in, you will not fail to get an answer.

Here are some suggestions and practical examples:

AIR This is the world of thoughts and words and numbers — through it you rise above pains and pleasure. If you find in yourself a lack of that element, dedicate some of your time to an abstract pursuit, with no other purpose in mind but the enjoyment of it. Go to art galleries, read books, play with your computer.

FIRE Feel the heat and warmth of the sun and the earth. Hold people's hands and feel their warmth.

WATER Make yourself slow right down; go for a walk outside in the early hours of the morning, when morning dew is still on the leaves. Be gentle with yourself, and as you look inside, feel for your inner spring of water. The world of emotions belongs to the water element; it cannot be forced, it can only be allowed.

EARTH Grounding is essential to feel secure and to be present. Do little things around the house, tend to the garden, watch your plants grow, play with the children... grounding is easy if you put yourself to it.

Everybody is different in their disposition of elements, and an imbalance in the disposition, for example, of water-air is not the same as an imbalance in the disposition fire-air. Tune in to your particular need, remember to always focus on the element you are lacking in and not on the one you feel overburdened with, as you will only end up fighting with it and blaming yourself for being the way you are. It is never a question of changing your nature but of helping the flow, and that is always best done by giving energy to the weaker parts, nourishing them and helping them grow.

Calling the Powers

THE BEGINNING CEREMONY

For practical and sequential reasons this ceremony is placed at the end of part one, but
successful execution does presuppose your
knowledge of what is explained in part two
(how to use your magical tools, the herbs,
flowers and stones). This is the opening ceremony of all magic and is to be repeated every
time you want to accomplish something by
magic. It is a ritual in which after giving your
thanks to existence, you open yourself to her
and ask for guidance. Your inner voice in this
moment will be strong and clear, and, answering to your pure intent, will set you on your
way.

Before commencing the actual incantation
call to your mind the reason why you have
invoked the elements — the reason for your
magic. If, for example, you need a magic to
help you find a new job, call this request in
your mind. If you already know what kind of
work you would like to do, you can see yourself
doing it, in a beautiful environment, with
happy people around you. Now hold that image
in your mind. If you don't yet know what kind
of job you would like to find, just hold your
wish in your mind. Hold the words or the
feelings or the images for at least one minute. It

can be difficult. If you loose it, just call it back
without getting annoyed about it. At this stage
much depends on your ability to hold something in your mind, undisturbed, for a period of
time.

After about one minute let it go. Relax and
wait for the answer. One of the elements will
present itself to you: that is the element you
must use as an environment for your magic. For
example, if the element answering you is fire,
you could use candles for your incantation or
your burner or an outside bonfire or the sun.

There are different ways in which the element may present itself to you: you might just
see it in your mind as the symbol standing in
front of you, or you might see it as it is free in
nature. You might find yourself reaching for
the cup and drinking out of it, or you might
suddenly notice the smoke of the incense filling
the room. The elements can answer in many
different ways!

The more you can concentrate while asking
your questions, the more detailed an answer
you will be able to get. You might be able to see
the whole incantation in all of its details: the
candles you want to burn, what color they are
and where you are to put them; the flowers
next to them, what type and color they are;
maybe even the words of the incantation which

Previous page
**The beginning ceremony. You will have prepared
incense for burning, wine in your cup, and a half-cup
of rice in your brass bowl before you begin this most
important of ceremonies — one in which you give
your thanks to existence and open yourself to her
guidance.**

will have to be pronounced or written down.

It is more likely that at the beginning you
will only get an indication as to what element
should be your choice for this matter. Consulting the table on page 79 you will see what
methods concord to that element. From your
study of the primary tools you will know that
herbs can help you very well in health and
beauty matters and everything that has to do
with the body; flowers with emotional issues;
and stones both with practical issues or ideas
and projects.

All you need to do now is to combine your
information in a simple and satisfactory way. In
part three there are many examples showing
ready-made incantations and rituals. They can
be followed and experimented with, if desired,
but they only want to be examples, indications
of what you can do by yourself. Magic is the
most creative activity that you can practice. It
is not to be copied. Even ancient rituals are
only actions which contain a certain message —
that message is what has been transferred on
from generation to generation, not the details
of the gestures, which in themselves are insig-
nificant.

When magic is reduced to the blind repetition of words and gestures it becomes a
mockery of itself. Magic is creativity. As you

learn to respect and watch nature with her
elements and tools, and learn to use them, they
can become an alphabet of letters with which
you can construct words in whatever formation
you please and like. Use the examples in part
three as a basis to make your own rituals. This
is the art of magic, the most free and fun
experience of mankind — that which puts man
directly and really in touch with the god in him:
the creator.

So, prepare yourself and your place. Choose
the time according to what kind of magic you
want to perform — see heading on "Times".
Cleanse and clothe yourself, and prepare yourself internally by relaxing and focusing your
energy. Gather the symbols of the elements and
your protector.

Facing east place the symbols in front of you
— the protector can be anywhere near you.
There can be music in the background if you
like, as long as it is one that helps you
concentrate. It is optional to cast the circle on
the ground — tracing it with chalk or white
flour but it is always obligatory to "complete"
yourself by casting your inner circle. Spend
enough time doing this, until you feel that your
energy is flowing strongly and unhindered.
Forget yourself in the visualization (or feeling)
of a strong flow of light circulating around you.

If some days it is particularly difficult to feel your inner circle, also do it externally, drawing the circle on the ground — that will certainly help you. But, remember, it is best not to proceed with the ritual if you cannot reach the required inner space of wholeness and completion. When you are ready open your eyes and softly gaze at the symbols of the four elements in front of you. Then close your eyes and see them again in your mind's eyes as they were before your open eyes. Do this a few times and you will find that your total attention and focus is on them.

You will have prepared burning incense, fire in your burner, wine in your cup and a half cupful of rice in your brass bowl. The incense you are burning can be a general purifying one or a more specific one according to the magic you wish to accomplish (see "Tools of Magic"). Take a handful of rice and throw it in the fire, drink enough wine to feel it wet in your mouth and descending inside you. While you are doing this acknowledge the elements. As you drink the wine, gaze at the incense floating through the air and say to yourself:

You are here and I thank you

AIR

You are here and I thank you

WATER

While you burn the rice, say to yourself:

You are here and I thank you

FIRE

You are here and I thank you

EARTH

The words don't have to be precisely those. Any word you really feel will do as long as you know you are acknowledging the presence of the element and paying your respects to it.

PART II

In Your Magic garden

From Earth my true home,
These herbs I welcome!
With their powers they will show,
In peace and love the way to go.

This section is dedicated to the study of three primary tools. As you know from part one a primary tool is a thing of nature which you come in close contact with, for the purpose of doing magic.

Three such tools are shown here; how to choose them, care for them and use them for magic is explained. Since your relationship to a primary tool is a very intimate and personal one, take this information to help you discover your own way of using primary tools.

Herbs, flowers and stones have been chosen because they are easy to find, to keep and to use. Together they also cover a wide range of possibilities and needs.

Herbs are down-to-earth and practical; they relate very well to the physical side of things. The magic of flowers is subtler and can deal more readily with the emotional sphere. Stones vibrate at a very low speed and connect easily with the spiritual side of things, that which transforms slowly and deeply, which is at the root of actions.

You might consider any situation on each of these three levels. You might choose to act on one, or two, or all three of them, depending on what your needs are at that moment.

For example, you want to find a new love: you can drink a potion to make you more desirable and irresistible or you can operate a flower incantation to open your heart and call the presence of another heart, or you could choose to use a stone that changes the pattern of your life from a state of living alone to the state of living together.

Perhaps you are concerned with your appearance. If you drink a herb potion it will make you healthier and more beautiful, while a flower incantation will help you love yourself and the way you look. A stone magic, instead, will act on the deeper self-image you have of yourself and help change that into a better one.

It depends on what you need. The three tools aid and integrate each other; it is easier to love one's own image when its appearance is better, and a deep change of perspective ensures a lasting improvement on your experience of it. Sometimes you will wish to use only herbs: perhaps you are going to a party, and wish to have success for that night. Sometimes flowers will answer your needs: you want to improve the connection with your lover or friend. Sometimes you feel a basic change is needed in your life and you appeal to stones. Sometimes, on very special occasions you will want to use all three tools at once. In this case you might also want to pay close attention to the times of the moon and the winds, and to

Stones may appear hard and un-alive but in fact, as you hold them you will begin to feel their connection and their ancient powers.

your preparation. If all these elements come together there is no saying where you will stop!

BEGINNING THE MAGIC WITH YOUR TOOLS

Using tools will not change the usual opening ritual that you have learned in part one, "Calling the Powers". All you need to do is to have them ready inside the circle, if you have drawn the circle on the ground, or in front of you together with the symbols of the elements.

The following is an example of the opening ritual using the tools.

TO IMPROVE CREATIVITY IN WORK

You have come to a point of change regarding

your working life; you are aware that it is not just a momentary discontent — you want to alter the content of your work; you want to be able to use more creatively the hours you spend working. Perhaps you feel you are ready to do so, and that this is the moment to make it happen.

Take the appropriate stone for the purpose, in this case the rutilated quartz. Sit in the circle and call the powers as explained in part one. As you formulate your wish and need, and focus your mind on it, pick up the stone and hold it in your left hand. One of the elements will call you. As you know, that is the element which will serve as background to your magic. In this case, let us say it is the element fire which answers you. This means that your working problem should be dealt with in the range of initiative, strength, passion, energy; applying initiative and strength you will obtain what you want.

You will now pass the stone from the left to the right hand. Your intuition will furnish you with the details of the incantation.

You know that the full moon gives a full blast of physical powers to your incantations (see heading on "Magical Times"). As this is a very important issue for you, you decide to wait until the next full moon. Wrap up the stone in

Hold the stone before the flames, close enough for the light to shine through. Allow the spirit of the stone and the flame to meet — let the warmth of one come to the coolness of the other. The quartz will shine and sparkle in the glow and will now hold within it your own needs.

---

a white cloth and keep it in your spell box until the appointed night.

That night cleanse and clothe yourself, prepare your place and concentrate. Light the burner and extinguish all electric lights and candles. Hold the stone in front of the flames, close enough that the light will shine on it, but without burning your fingers. Sit silently and let the spirit of the stone and that of the fire meet and let the stone be warmed up by the fire. The quartz will shine and sparkle in the warm glow. The stone now holds your need. The fire will provide it with the right energy to answer it.

Carry your stone to work; perhaps you can place it on your desk, or keep it in your handbag or in your pocket (in this case wrap it up in soft cloth). From this moment on situations will present themselves where you can use your creativity, perhaps in the form of a new assignment, or a change of environment. You will see yourself reacting to them with passion, whereby previously you might have ignored them. Keep the stone with you until you feel that the need is not there anymore. Following this pattern you can use any of the primary tools, for any need.

At the beginning, when perhaps you don't trust yourself enough to choose the details of the incantation, you can follow the suggestions which are given for each tool about ways of using them in magic. The following chart presents them in brief for a quick consultation. Remember, though, to be flexible and to use your own initiative when you are in doubt.

The elements and the primary tools are given a graphic symbol (like the timing factors). These are then repeated later in the book for each magical ritual for quick reference.

HERBS	AIR		Dreams	Place the appropriate herb under your pillow. Ask for a revealing dream.
	FIRE		Bonfire	Burn the herbs while you pronounce your bidding and hold it in your mind.
	WATER		Bathroom	Throw the herbs in the bath and lie in it, visualize the wish coming true.
	EARTH		Nature	Take the appropriate herb, sit under a tree and drink an infusion of it (if it is a drinkable one). Formulate your need.
FLOWERS	AIR		Visualization	Visualize the flower becoming larger and encompassing you.
	FIRE		Sun	Wear the flower's essence and let the sun exalt its perfume. Pronounce your wish.
	WATER		Seaside	Throw the flower in the sea (or watercourse) expressing your wish.
	EARTH		Routine actions	Fill the place you are working in with the required flower.
STONES	AIR		Spell	Write the spell on a parchment and put it away together with the stone.
	FIRE		Candle	Lay the stone near a candle, and leave it there until the candle is extinguished.
	WATER		Well	Rinse yourself with the well-water in which the stone has been lying for three hours.
	EARTH		Keeping	Keep the stone on your body, in a pouch, for the required time.

ALL-TIME MAGIC

In ancient times, when man hunted and woman gathered, the only wisdom and healing power came from the earth in the form of herbs and plants. The one (usually the woman) who held the knowledge of them, ranked high in the tribe, and this knowledge was transmitted verbally from mother to daughter. In such times medicine and magic were one and the same thing, and even in later periods of history, such as in ancient Greece, Rome and Egypt, the two were still closely linked. In Greece, the word *pharmakeia* from which the modern word pharmacy derives, meant both the compounding of medicinal drugs and the making of magical potions and philters. Even as late as the Middle Ages, when modern medicine was in its early years of trial and error, it was to the local witch, with her knowledge of herbs and potions, that poor folk would go; and she would certainly kill fewer people than the medicine man with his leeches and saws.

The village witch was then "herbalist, spellmaker, interpreter of dreams, healer, midwife and psychologist all rolled into one" (*ABC of Witchcraft*, D. Valiente). And it was from the herbs that she gained much of her power. Herbs are a perfect example of what real magic

is all about. By learning to listen to herbs and by talking to them, it is possible to create a relationship with them which will enable us to use their powers to an extent that far exceeds what can be achieved by science.

Herb's magic operates on a very immediate level, that of sensations. Its effects, although acting on a transient plane, open the door to long lasting changes but can be very useful as quick remedies too. For example, rue will open your eyes to mistakes which you might be

In the most remote times woman found her wisdom and healing powers in the earth in the form of herbs, plants and flowers. Medicine and magic were the same and provided by nature, direct from the source. In the realms of science man has forgotten this simple truth — that the world we inhabit can provide everything we need if we know where to look and how to listen.

to be studied very carefully in their own realm, and that is the realm of the physical. This means that you must observe them, gather information about them and experiment with them. If you feel attracted to herbs and want to use them as primary tools you will need patience, time and dedication.

Buy a good herbal and flick through its pages — you are bound to be already acquainted with some herbs and plants. If you live in the country you might want to go around and see if you can recognize any. If you are a town dweller, and really cannot afford the time for a trip to the countryside (that is always best), go to a local nursery and browse around. It would be best of all if you could find someone — a friend, an acquaintance, maybe just a student of alternative medicine and homeopathy who would be more than happy to talk about his own subject — who knows herbs and can take you around vegetable gardens and fields and point them out to you.

Once you have decided on the ones you are interested in for the moment, you must carefully study their properties and medicinal uses in your herbal. Our foremothers were born with this knowledge passed on to them through generations — they knew instinctively which herb to drink, which to apply on wounds — but

committing at the present time. This herb magic will not change those mistakes, or the reasons for which you are committing them, but it will bring your attention to them and act as a stepping stone towards a deeper understanding and change, and it will certainly be very useful at that moment.

GETTING TO KNOW THEM

If you want to do magic with herbs, they need

we have lost this knowledge and studying the herb is part of the process of recalling it. Some herbs might be dangerous used in the wrong way — and you would not want to learn by experience.

Also learn, if you can, what the history of the herb is and what legends and traditions are attached to its name. It is a bit like asking somebody you have just met about their life in the last few years. It might not be at all relevant to your connection to them — but it might still help you to get to know that person.

Finally, use your own intuition and experi-ment. For example, if you feel that witch hazel is the herb of seduction — and consulting your herbal you see that there is nothing against using it in contact with the skin — throw it in the bath and visualize yourself being irresistible in the particular occasion you are preparing yourself for. As usual it is most important that you concentrate and put your whole intensity behind it. Probably while you are in the bath you will also have an intuition of what to wear to enhance your seductiveness, what make-up to use, what part of yourself to emphasize.

If the herb is not working, if it is really

Left
Getting to know your plants and herbs is a most important part of magic — getting to know them as friends. Even the scientists nowadays acknowledge that plant life has some strong response to human presence. The better you know your plants the better they will work with you.

Below
The pestle and mortar were always basic tools of all alchemists and pharmacists — they bring the energy of the body directly, through natural tools, into the grain or herbal cures. They are your essential tools as a magic maker, to create all powders.

totally the wrong one, you will already feel it when you are still in the bath — you will be put off and irritable. You will miss that rush of energy which comes from vibrating in tune with the universe, the feeling which tells you that the magic is working. Put it down to experience and try again. You will not err much. If you have chosen herbs, they have chosen you — and your intuition will guide you safely.

A chart of some select herbs and the magic related to them is enclosed in this section. If you want to you can start by experimenting with those.

USING HERBS IN MAGIC

When you are going to do magic in which you will use an herb, or herbs, first of all you need to prepare them beforehand.

If the herb is one which needs to be in powder form for that magic, powder it and place it in a small bowl which you have kept for that purpose. Or you might need to cut a sprig of the herb in order to prepare an infusion, which you will then pour into the cup ready for the magic. Or you might simply need to take a few pinches of the required herb(s) out of their containers and place them in the small bowl to be put inside the circle.

Always take into consideration the medicinal nature of the herb — you would not, of course, drink an infusion of a poisonous herb, and you should prefer a relaxing one such as camomile when you are over-excited, and one for vitality when you feel tired. Herbs can be prepared as follows:

As POTIONS Infusions of one or more herbs (sometimes other ingredients are added such as petals of flowers, fruits, peels, etc.).

As POWDERS To be sprinkled in the wind

(wait for the right wind to raise) or on parts of the body or of the room.

CAN BE BURNED   By throwing them into the burner or into a bonfire outside.

CAN BE KEPT   By placing them in a sachet, and kept on one's person for a time, or kept under the pillow (specially for dream magic), or placed in the apposite spell box, together with a few written words of power.

IN THE BATH   Can be thrown into the bath water to make a deliciously toning and relaxing magic. Specially good in preparing for important occasions.

PRACTICAL INFORMATION

An infusion is made by combining boiling water and the plants, usually the green parts or the flowers, and steeping them to extract the active ingredients. The usual amounts are half an ounce or one ounce to one pint of water. Usually the hot water is poured over the herb. Sometimes it is advisable to throw the herbs into the boiling pot and to remove the pot immediately from the fire. The steeping time is about ten minutes. Strain to drink and add honey or sugar if needed.

A decoction is used for bark, roots, seeds, etc., which usually need to boil to release their active ingredients. Boil half an ounce plant parts per one cup of water; boil for three to four minutes, unless otherwise indicated.

A powder is obtained by grinding the dry herb with a mortar and pestle until you have obtained a powder. Keep the enamel pot and the mortar and pestle which you will be using for your magic herbs separated from the rest of your kitchen utensils. Perhaps you can keep them on the shelf or drawer in which you keep your dried herbs for magic.

GATHERING YOUR HERBS

If some herbs grow abundantly around where you live, you can simply gather them fresh every time you need them. Hawthorn bushes, for example, are everywhere in the English countryside which is green and full of luscious plants.

Even though it is in the best witches' tradition to gather herbs in the moonlight — a waxing moon for white magic, a black moon for an evil one — I advise you to go during the daytime hours and to leave home early enough not to be caught by darkness while still working. Recognizing the right herbs is already difficult, and darkness and cold would not improve things.

herbs on a shelf which will be for these herbs only. The shelf can be in your magic place, if you have one, or in another quiet room. But, please, not in the kitchen. The temptation to reach over for your magic thyme while cooking the Sunday roast might be too strong to resist!

CONSECRATING HERBS, SEEDS AND OTHER TOOLS

This is one consecrating ritual which is very useful for all new herbs, tools and implements; all these things which newly enter your magic life. (For more specific consecrating needs — for example, when you need to consecrate a particular potion prior to drinking it — address yourself directly to the element of your magic at that moment. For example, if you need to consecrate an infusion to give you power, you might want to appeal yourself directly to the element fire.)

Prepare yourself for magic and gather the symbols of the elements. For this ritual, in the cup you will have prepared some water with a pinch of sea salt in it (it must be pure source water — you can buy it bottled or fetch it from a natural source if you live out of town). Place the object or objects which you want to consecrate in front of you, between you and the

Bring with you a boleen or any small sharp knife to cut the leaves and branches and herbs you will need, and a basket to put them in. As you cut them, wrap up the same ones in a sheet of thin paper. Otherwise, you will have a hard time separating the various species once you are home. If it is summer and the sun is hot, be sure to wear a hat!

BUYING THEM DRY

Probably, specially at the beginning when you are not too sure of what they are supposed to look like, you will buy most of your herbs dry from your local herbalist.

The dry herbs which you buy will be consecrated and kept in the appropriate containers. Some will be in ceramic or glass jars, some in paper or linen bags. Keep your dried

Naturally the very best way to make your connection with plants and herbs — to make them "want" to work with you — is to grow them yourself. The best place is a garden, with a space set aside for the magic herbs and plants, but even if you live twenty floors up in an apartment building, the same applies — grow them yourself and they will become your friends.

---

symbols of the elements. If you have marked the circle on the ground and the symbols are at the four points of the circle, sit facing east and place the object to consecrate in front of you. With your eyes closed, relax and concentrate for a few minutes. When your mind is still and all other concerns have left you for the time being, with your left hand take the plant, or seed or whatever object you want to consecrate, hold it over the incense and say:

This air to make you free

Now hold the object over the burner in which a small flame will be burning and say:

This fire to give you life

Then, still holding the object in your left hand, with the right sprinkle the salted water over it and say:

This water to purify

Finally, take a few pinches of rice (or wheat or earth depending on what you use to symbolize the element earth) out of your brass bowl, spill them on the ground in front of you and lay the object to rest over it. Say:

This earth to let you be

As you say that, come to a kneeling position and bend forward letting your forehead touch the ground. In this abandoned posture feel the earth accepting and welcoming you and your object and feel the presence of your object in the home of your spirit.

GROWING YOUR HERBS

INSIDE All said and done, by far the best thing to do if you want to know herbs, is to grow a few yourself. It is very good if you happen to have a garden and can dedicate part of it to the growth of herbs for magic, but even if you live in town on the twentieth floor of a sky-scraper in a studio apartment, you can still make your own little indoor herb garden. All you need is a few pots, some soil and a corner of the room under a window where the sun visits for at least a couple of hours a day. (A sun lamp, such as many use to give artificial sunlight to the plants, in this case, will not serve the purpose. If the herbs are to develop their magic potential they do need some natural sunlight.)

There is indeed no better way to get to know a plant than to grow it, and all the attention

Your working implements should be kept together in a
safe, clean place and used only for the magic garden.
Any other gardening work should not entail the use of
these tools.

and care you will have given it to help it transform from seed to herb will come back a thousandfold to you when you perform your incantations.

Consecrate your seed before planting, and when the little plant for the first time makes an appearance outside the earth, welcome it to its new life. Don't worry about seeming ridiculous, talking to your plants. Man used to "talk" to the vegetable world long before he was able to communicate with his own kind.

If you have your own magic place of course the indoor garden should be kept there.

A few herbs which can be easily home grown are listed in this chapter. You can try those or any other variety that best fits you. When you are growing indoors, always remember to put a vaporizer next to the central heating as excessive dryness in the atmosphere will damage the plants.

OUTSIDE   If you do have a spot of garden or land anywhere, you can make it into your own private altar of nature. Two or three square meters of land will do quite well for your first herb garden. Choose a piece of land where the earth looks moist and rich. Don't worry, however, if what you have available is not perfect; you can always better it by adding new earth and fertilizer.

LOCATION

Preferably choose a spot close to a single tree. It should be a tree of age and stature that can cast a shadow over your garden; some of your herbs will not want to be in direct sunlight. An ash tree would be perfect. It is said that ashes were favorites of old-time witches and that they used the wood for their broomsticks. If you stand close to an ash in a night of full moon and see the silvery leaves shine under the moon, you will be able to understand the mystique of this tree.

Having chosen your location, it is best to clearly define the edges of the allotment. For this purpose you should use hawthorn bushes (*Crataegus oxyacantha*). Perhaps you can buy them already big in the plant nursery, or transplant them from the wild where they grow in abundance. Hawthorn had a bad reputation in the Middle Ages, when it was thought to be used by witches for evil deeds. But it is a very beneficial plant, which can keep the good energy of your magic herb garden enclosed in serenity.

PREPARATION

To set up the garden first consult a calendar

and chose the time when the moon is again growing. It does not have to be a full moon as long as it is in its waxing phase.

If you can, wait for a west wind to raise. A windsock can tell you when the time has come. It is good to start a herb garden under the influence of the west wind, as it is a moist and fertile force which will ensure the richness of your land's product.

IMPLEMENTS

A RAKE   A rake is needed to clean the surface of stones and weeds and to aerate the ground. Work on the surface and be careful of the smaller plants. This needs to be done often.

A HOE   You will need a good hoe for turning the soil — once or twice a year depending on the culture. You will turn the soil

Below and right
Within a seed, everything that the plant will have already exists and so planting for magic must be undertaken with great reverence, an action of birth. It is always best to keep your seeds in a linen bag — natural fibres for retaining the natural energies of the seeds.

so that the lower layers are exposed to the air and the weeds are eliminated. You can also turn in fertilizer and dung at this point as well as new good earth if needed.

A WINDSOCK   This should be kept somewhere in your garden plot so that you can always tell what kind of wind is blowing. Sometimes you will need to know this for your incantations, and the garden is the best place to keep it.

A BOLEEN   A boleen is a small sickle-shaped knife which you will use to cut the herbs.

A WATERING CAN   An ordinary metal watering can is better in this case than a modern plastic one or a hose, metal being a primary element and therefore preferable for channeling magic.

Always use water from a natural source such as a nearby stream, pond or well. Especially tap water is not recommended.

Your implements need to be kept together in a safe, clean place. They must be used only for this magical garden. If you have another garden also, then be sure to keep your implements separately. Also greet tools of your magic when you pick them up, and thank them for helping you when you put them down. It is important that you remember to do this *every time*, as that

will increase their power by and by, so that the day will soon come when simply touching them will charge you with positive and constructive energy.

SEEDS, SEEDING AND CUTTING

Within a seed all the possibilities of your plant are already present so that when you are seeding for magic you are undertaking a most important action, something to be done with great reverence.

Every plant has its own seeding time which must be adhered to. Until that time keep your seeds for magic in a muslin bag tied with silk.

Each bag must contain seeds of one species only; moreover you can also separate those seeds which you are going to use for a particular purpose. For example, if you are going to use some particular herbs in an incantation to help conceive a baby girl, you will unite all the bags containing the seeds of the relevant herbs in one bigger bag of the appropriate color (in this case pink) and you will add to the bag whatever other spells or amulets you want to use.

Make sure that all your seeds are healthy before you plant them. A healthy seed is dry, hard, quite large and of a good lustrous color. If it has ridges or spots don't use it, as you can imagine what disastrous effect a spoiled plant could bring to your incantations.

It used to be said that witches would gather and seed their plants in darkness on a full moon night, when practicing white magic, or on a black moon night when they were up to no good! In fact, planting a seed in the earth, while the full moon shines upon you, can be a very romantic and fascinating operation.

However, whether you seed during the day or during the night, always choose a period when the moon is waxing, as this helps all growing matters. All seeds should be consecrated before seeding. (See consecrating ritual above).

Garlic, the famous, strong-flavored herb is easy to grow inside or outside and forms the very best of good luck charms in magic.

The cutting of the herbs is also important. Make sure to only use your consecrated boleen for the task. They should be cut at the right time; since that time is different for each plant, your herbal book will help you with this. Take only the healthy and intact parts of the plant. Put them together in bunches of a few and hang them to dry (unless otherwise required).

WHAT YOU CAN GROW

Here I have chosen a few herbs, some of which you all know and have used dozens of times; you will now have the chance to look at them with different eyes.

Partly by yourself, using your own intuition and awareness, and partly by consulting your herbal, you will be able to grow and use any number of other herbs which you feel pulled by, and which you might like to experiment with. These herbs can be grown in your own magic garden, or on your windowsill or balcony, or in your indoor garden, taking the measures described above.

GARLIC
Allium sativum

Everybody must be familiar with this strongly

flavored herb and with his history as a magical plant. Who doesn't know about garlic and ghosts?

Garlic can easily be home grown, in your little magical garden, inside or outside. Plant the little bulbs in furrows at about thirty centimeters one from the other (in separate pots if it is indoors). Use humid, fertilized soil. Plant in October and you'll have fresh products in spring.

MEDICINAL PROPERTIES Garlic relieves various problems associated with poor digestion. Also regularizes the action of the liver and gall bladder. It is beneficial for the blood circulation and heart action, and it is helpful in intestinal infections. The bulb is the part used medicinally.

NAME AND HISTORY *Allium* takes its name from Celtic *all*, hot, burning, related to the taste of the plant, and *sativum*, which is a contraction from Latin *seminativum*, seedable, that which can be planted.

In Egypt garlic was given to the laborers who built the pyramids for strength and nourishment; in ancient Rome garlic was given also to the laborers and to soldiers who ate it before battle (maybe in hand to hand combat its smell scared the enemies away!). It was dedicated to Mars the god of war. Because of its strong antiseptic properties it was believed to ward off all evils.

MAGICAL PROPERTIES AND USES Garlic is the good luck charm par excellence. Together with mandrake, which is the same kind of charm but of a softer energy, they can protect any household through all kinds of changes to progress toward the good of all involved. Garlic has a strong, male energy, and will ensure that the strength required for any situation will always be there.

To use garlic, call the power fire in your Beginning the Magic ritual. Hold the garlic in both your hands and keep it in front of the fire for a few seconds with your eyes closed. Listen to your heart beat and feel strength permeate your body. Hang the magic garlic in your kitchen, or on the patio, or anywhere in your house that is convenient. Be careful that it does not get mixed up with the garlic you use for cooking! Change your garlic charm when it becomes too dry or mouldy. Once the garlic is so treated you can use it anytime for strength and power giving incantations.

THYME
Thymus vulgaris

Very common, nice smelling plant, which can

Thyme works well to disinfect the digestive system, and generally tones up the whole physical system, stimulating the appetite.

be easily home grown. Seed in box in March and transplant to pot or garden in May. Give it calcareous and clayey soil. Cut during flowering time in May-July.

MEDICINAL PROPERTIES   Thyme disinfects the digestive and respiratory apparatus, tones the entire system and stimulates the appetite and the digestion; therefore it is used for throat and bronchial problems, for gastritis and lack of appetite. It is also used as a mouthwash, and to make a purifying face mask. In the bath water it improves bruises, swellings and sprains. The whole herb is used.

NAME AND HISTORY   The name thyme comes from the Greek *thymia* which means perfume. In the Middle Ages it was believed that sleeping on a pillow stuffed with thyme would dispel melancholy. It was also believed to inspire courage. According to another legend at midnight on midsummer's night, the king of the fairies and his followers dance on beds of wild thyme.

MAGICAL PROPERTIES AND USES   This is indeed a rich herb! The sweet scent and the abundance of magical and medicinal properties, make thyme one of the most precious plants.

Use thyme above all to prepare yourself for magic. The scent of thyme has the property of gathering a person's energies and of focusing

Angelica is really only for the outside, as it can grow to seven feet in height. The parts of the plant used for magic though, are the roots, rootstock and seeds which can be gathered in the second year of growth.

them in the immediate space and time, thus increasing the person's strength in that moment. This is a strength which is not the raw force needed to overcome difficulties (for that use garlic), but is rather a fragrance of awareness of the situation and therefore of the key needed to unlock it. Use by throwing a few sprigs of the herb (fresh is better, but dry will do) in the bath water, during the cleansing ritual before magic.

ANGELICA
Angelica archangelica

This plant can grow quite tall, from three to seven feet high; therefore you should grow it only if you do have an outside garden. As it has strong magical powers I have included it in the detailed list, even though it might not look very pretty in your little garden.

To seed this plant you must have fresh seeds, which you will have kept in water for three nights around the time of full moon (the night before, the same night, the night after), in a bowl outside, so that they can become charged with her rays. Seed in spring and transplant in autumn, putting the little plants in a circle, at one meter one from the other. This plant needs a humid climate to grow properly.

MEDICINAL PROPERTIES The parts used medicinally are the rootstock, roots and seeds, which are gathered in the second year of growth. They are aromatic and digestive. Although angelica is a stimulant if taken in very small doses, it is a depressant at a higher dosage. An infusion of the fresh plant (100g in 1l of water) added to the bath water makes a very relaxing bath.

NAME AND HISTORY The name of this plant comes from the Greek *agghelos* which means announcer. Therefore angel means announcer from god, because in the Middle Ages it was believed that angelica had been given by god to a monk in a dream to combat the plague. William Coles said in 1656 that if the roots of angelica were carried about a man he would be protected from evil: "contagious aire ingendring pestilence/infects not those that in the mouth have ta'en angelica, that happy counterbane." (*The Magic of Herbs*, C.F. Leyel, 1932).

MAGICAL PROPERTIES AND USES It is more than likely that in those times, like today, some people had become attuned to angelica's magical powers of bringing the angelic quality of temperance to people. That is, the capacity of rising above the present troubles and of being able to wait serenely for the outcome of the events. The antiseptic and tonic medicinal qualities must have done the rest to make people believe that it was god given.

For magic gather the roots in September-October, possibly waiting for a west wind to blow, and dry them in the sun. Prepare an elixir in this way: 8g of roots, 40g of sugar, 100g of alcohol, enough water to reach 1l in all. Add a slice of the well-washed peel of the season's first fruit, and leave to steep for ten days. Filter, add more sugar and water. It is ready. Use it in those incantations when you need to call the gift of temperance on you.

A quick magic tip: once you have so prepared the elixir of temperance and have consecrated it by using it the first time with the whole ritual of Calling the Powers, keep it somewhere very protected from outside interferences. In times of need you can just take a sip of it, and you will immediately feel the magical benefits.

ROSEMARY
Rosmarinus officinalis

Grow this happy herb and you will always have a good friend with you. Seed it in May in a covered box, and transplant it when the herb has taken. Give it a sandy soil and plenty of attention.

MEDICINAL PROPERTIES Rosemary is aromatic, digestive, antiseptic, stimulant and antispasmodic. Thanks to all these properties it is widely used both for internal and external purposes. The branches with leaves are the parts used.

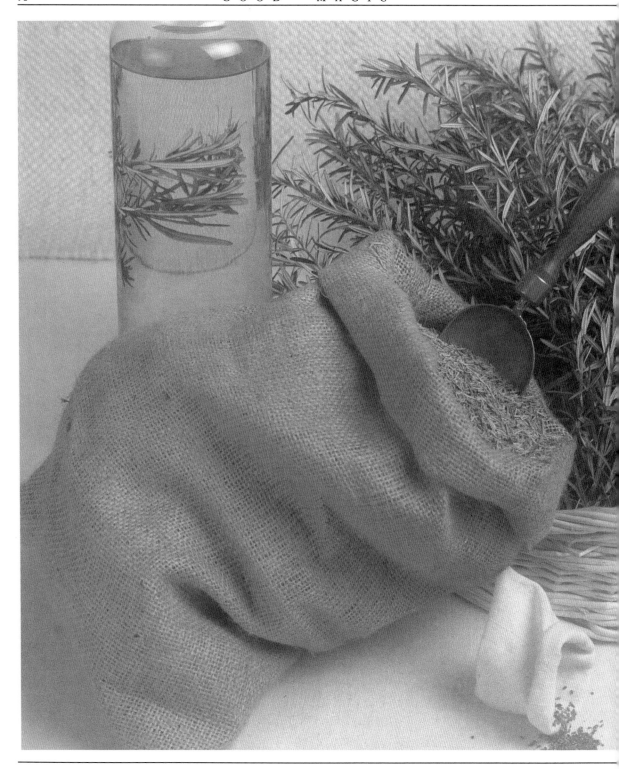

Rosemary means "dew of the sea" and brings openness to that part of you which is child-like and innocent, so potentially very happy. A strong and yet delicate plant — like the dew of the sea.

NAME AND HISTORY *Rosmarinus* comes from the Latin *ros*, dew, and *marinus*, sea; therefore the name means dew of the sea. The herb, in fact, grows spontaneously by the seaside. Rosemary has always been associated with remembrance, happy memories, fidelity and love and has always been used amply in witchcraft, bringing many legends with its history. One such is that a rosemary plant which flourishes outside a house gives a sure sign that the woman is boss of that household! Another states that a man who is not sensitive to the scent of rosemary will never be able to truly love a woman. Rosemary was also believed to have exorcising qualities and was often used to cleanse people and places of evil spirits.

MAGICAL PROPERTIES AND USES   This herb has the property of opening your heart to that part of it which is still childlike and innocent, therefore bringing happiness and contentment. Its name, "seadew" expresses well its magical qualities, strong and yet delicate and innocent.

By opening a connection with rosemary you will receive the very precious gift of contentment. Although it will be in the form of a temporary experience — as is the case with all herbs' magic — this feeling will make a lasting impression on you and will help you find ways to make that experience a lasting one. Use it

Wormwood can begin its life indoors but will eventually have to be re-planted outside as the final growth may be as long as two meters. Plant in March at the time of the new moon and transplant when the seed has taken. An infusion of this plant will bring enthusiasm and energy after magic work has slightly depleted your energy.

every time you feel you have lost contact with the child within you; every time the seriousness of everyday life, work, family problems, etc. are depressing you and you feel tired and uninspired.

Cut the little branches of your plant at the time of sunset, and hang them upside down in bunches to dry. Keep a sprig of the herb in your baby's room and you will ensure a safe and happy growth for him or her.

For your own magic, prepare a potion by mixing an infusion of rosemary (1g in 100ml of water) with an infusion of thyme (same amounts). Drink slowly when you are ready inside the circle (the circle will be either drawn on the ground or completed inside yourself). Another way of using rosemary is to add it to the bath water prior to magic rituals, either with thyme or without.

WORMWOOD
Artemisia absinthium

This is another useful herb to grow, which can also be adapted to an indoor garden. It can grow up to two meters long, by which time you had better transplant it outside!

Plant it in March, in a covered box. Wait to do that until the new moon. Transplant when

the seed has taken, in the garden or in a pot. Give it a sandy soil and plenty of light.

MEDICINAL PROPERTIES The leaves and the flowery tops are the parts of this plant used medicinally. It stimulates the nervous system and gives vitality and appetite, thus helping the liver and the stomach in their functions. It must be used with caution as it can be dangerous.

NAME AND HISTORY The name *artemisa* comes from the Greek *artemis*, good and healthy, referring to the beneficial properties of the plant, and *apsinthion*, not liked, because of its bitter taste. In the Middle Ages wormwood was recommended for magical practices. It was believed that a sprig of the herb hanging from the ceiling would preserve the house from evil. Yet in the Bible this herb is called to represent all sins in the world because of its unpleasant taste.

MAGICAL PROPERTIES AND USES Wormwood makes a very good infusion to drink after magic. It is a herb which gives vitality and enthusiasm, and therefore can help overcome low energy moments and can be helpful after performing incantations when you might have spent a lot more of your energies than you realized at the moment. Wormwood is also the right herb to use when you need the last bout of energy to finish a difficult task.

To prepare a magic potion of vitality make an infusion of the flowers and leaves, consecrate it to earth and drink it when needed. This potion can be very helpful during a long night of passion!

SAGE
Salvia officinalis

This herb can be easily home grown, in the garden or in a pot. Seed it in spring in a covered box and transplant it when it has taken. Give it a sandy soil and full sunlight. There are no particular magic requirements for the growing of this herb.

MEDICINAL PROPERTIES Sage stimulates the activity of the intestine and has a balsam effect on the respiratory system. It is digestive and aromatic, antispasmodic, anti-inflammatory, tonic and astringent. The parts used are the leaves and the flowery tops.

NAME AND HISTORY The name *salvia* comes from the Latin *salvare*, to heal, for the curative properties of the plant. Sage was very highly considered in the Middle Ages, so much so that it was believed it could defeat death. This was partly due to her antiseptic qualities which enabled some who rubbed it on their skin to escape the contagion of the plague. Contrary to rosemary, it was said that when sage is flourishing outside a house, it is the man who is the boss of the household.

MAGICAL PROPERTIES AND USES Sage has various different uses in magic, as its properties are of more than one kind.

The first, indisputable one, is to promote health. Sage used magically will give an immediate and strong feeling of health and well-being. It will furthermore indicate to you with dreams or images what you need to do in order to

The parts of sage to be used are the leaves and the flowery tops — for digestive stimulation of the intestines and a balsam effect on the respiratory system. The name comes from the Latin word meaning to heal.

acquire a perfect health. It will not tell you how to defeat death — as they believed in the Middle Ages — no herb can. But it can show you the ways in which you are currently courting a premature end to the well-being of your body.

Use it in this aspect when you are feeling unwell, of course, but also when you have a lot of energy and you feel you would like to improve the potential of your body. Make an infusion and drink during the Calling the Powers ritual. Athletes and sportsmen will benefit by keeping a sprig of dried sage in a muslin bag in a special box in their magic place, if they have one, or in a private room.

This is another interesting use of the herb sage: it will give the woman who uses it in the right way a glimpse of the kind of man (or male energy) which she would benefit most from. For this purpose, powder a dry sprig of sage in a night of waxing moon. Place the powder in your special box and wait till the moon has reached its course and it is full. Prepare yourself for magic, gather the symbols and call the element fire. You will then throw three pinches of the dried sage powder into the burner and ask the sage to reveal to you the furthering aspects of male energy. It might take the form of the image of a face in your mind, or

that of an activity or of an aspect of someone you know which you had previously over-looked.

This magic can be specially helpful if you are looking for a male partner, to help you make the right choice (you never know!), or if you feel your female energy needs to be balanced out by a stronger aspect of the male one.

For those who enjoy or suffer great rages of temper — mint cools and brings an evenness of spirit and mood. Good for jealousy, rashness and anger, this herb is truly enchanting.

MINT
Mentha piperita

Seed this fragrant herb in the spring, and transplant it in autumn if you have a garden. Any kind of soil will do for it, and it will be happy to have at least a few hours of sun every day. Mint planted for magic necessitates a west wind at the time of seeding if it is to fully develop her magical properties, and it fares best if it is closer to the west corner of your herb garden.

MEDICINAL PROPERTIES   Mint is a good all-round herb with many properties. It is tonic, digestive and helps the nerves and nerve-related problems. It also has a mildly analgesic function. It is antiseptic. The parts used are the leaves and the flowery tops.

NAME AND HISTORY   From the Latin *mens*, mind, because it was believed that mint had the power to fortify the intelligence. And *piperita*, from latin *piperatus*, peppery. Ancient Greeks named the plant *ketus* and dedicated it to Ares (Mars), god of war and to those who died in battle. From the Middle Ages some very strange incantations using mint have come to us, such as: "If your bees are dying, put some mint preparation in the beehive, and in a couple of hours they will be well".

MAGICAL PROPERTIES AND USES   The magical property of mint is to bring coolness and an even temper; very useful when you are burning with rage and would like to break everything to pieces!

Mint is really an enchanting and helpful tool in magic as it is of invaluable help in all those incantations where you are dealing with problems issuing from an excess of heat. That is jealousy, rashness, anger, etc. While the passions burn too hot it really is impossible to see the reality of the situation. Mint here works wonders. Drinking the potion during the ritual will enable you to see things how they really are. While the powers of the herb will not last very long, the understanding you have gained will, and you can then act on a more solid basis — having actually seen beyond the heated screen of your passions.

The best method for using mint is to make an infusion, consecrate it to the element water and drink it immediately before or during the incantation you are performing to solve your hot temper problem.

For example, you need to do a magic to help you with a situation which is making you exceedingly angry. Prepare an infusion of mint; prepare yourself for magic and call the element water to consecrate your potion; do it by

holding the cup, with both your hands, slightly above your head. Then, drink the potion slowly — as you feel the liquid descending in your body, imagine a wave of freshness descending with it. Say these words out loud:

Mint, your help I call! Fresh and peaceful your spirit comes!

Let the powers of mint cool your heart and soon you will feel your passions evaporate and you will be able to discern the real shape of the situation. Maybe you will see that it was a question of a misunderstanding or a matter of insecurity or of unrealistic expectations. Now that you clearly determine what the real problem is, you can choose the magic most appropriate for your problem. Call the elements again and see which one answers you. Again choose one of the tools — or none at all — and create the incantation.

There is a certain strangeness about the mandrake — its resemblance to the human body and its Latin name *mandragora* which sounds somehow slightly sinister! In fact the name means "sleep substance" due to the narcotic effect of the root. It can also be called Satan's apple! All the old witches' covens take great delight in this root — for our purposes it need not have any sinister significance but simply good uses.

A quick magic tip: carry a sprig of dried mint with you and inhale the scent when you are loosing your temper: in a traffic jam, in the office, at home. Mint is a good magical ally.

For the following herbs growing instructions are not given. These herbs can be purchased dried from a herbalist or, where indicated, they can be gathered in the wild.

MANDRAKE
European: Mandragora officinarum

The mandrake root, which sometimes resembles a human figure, is available in herbal shops. Keep it in a paper bag, and put it in an aired place (not in a box).

MEDICINAL PROPERTIES   The medicinal part is the rootstock. Its use today is limited to homeopathic preparations for hay fever, asthma and cough.

NAME AND HISTORY   The word *mandragora* comes from the Sanskrit words *mangros* and *agora* meaning together sleep substance, because of the narcotic effect of the root. The European mandrake is also called Satan's apple.

It was used in ancient times as an anesthetic for surgery, as a sleeping pill when in pain and also as a remedy for melancholy. It was believed to promote conception.

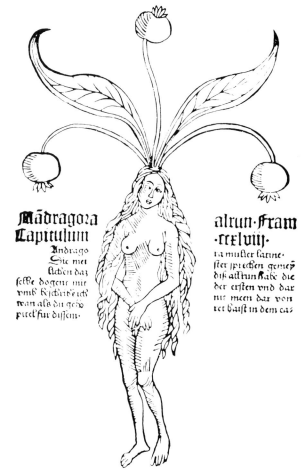

The mandrake has been considered a mystic plant since primitive times. In the Middle Ages, if the owner would be found having one, he or

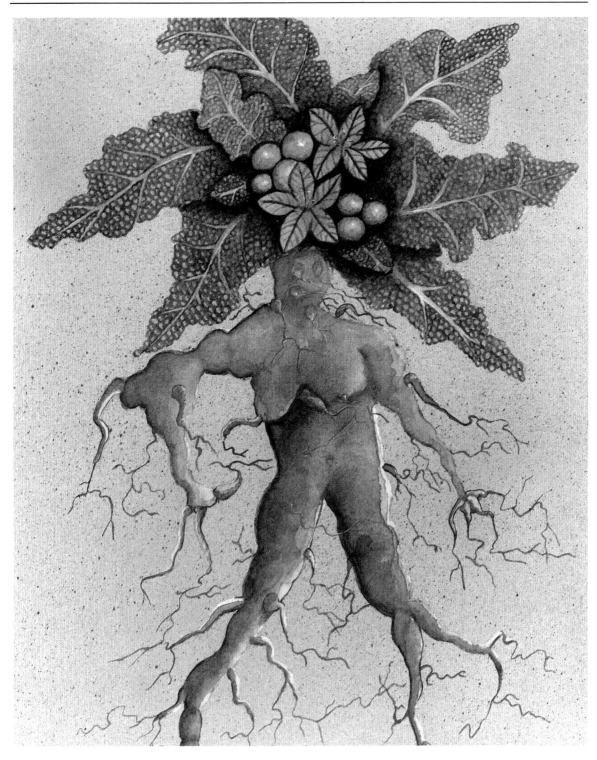

Used in the preparation of alcoholic drinks, rue is best known in natural circles for its normalizing effect on menstruation. In any event this herb is not to be used or taken in large doses.

she could be accused of witchcraft. The mandrake was in fact the medieval witches' most potent plant, capable of working every spell.

MAGICAL PROPERTIES AND USES *Mandragora*, today like yesterday, is a very powerful charm. If you can find a whole one which resembles a human figure, you can assign to it every job, and it will do it. It is a bit like the wild card of herbal magic.

Carry it with you in any situation where you need the help of the stars, and you will be lucky. Use it in any other magic, in conjunction with other practices, and you will have increased possibilities of success. Touching your root when you feel anxious or tense, will immediately bring you at ease. Giving such a root as a present to a friend means a lot!

RUE
Ruta graveolens

This is an aromatic herb which is used in the preparation of alcoholic drinks. Taken in very small doses it has the property of favoring the normalization of the menstrual flow in women. Once it was also used to provoke abortions, but the necessary dose for that is very close to the lethal dose, and it often caused the death of the women who tried it. The juice and the pulp of the plant can also be very irritating when they come into contact with the skin.

MEDICINAL PROPERTIES Once they were used to remove warts, but even that practice resulted quite harmful. Rue should not be used medicinally without the supervision of a doctor. Also, when using it for magic one must be very careful not to absorb the plant, either by drinking it or by putting it in close contact with the skin.

The parts of this plant used medicinally are the tops; they are mostly used to cure palpitations in women going trough menopause.

NAME AND HISTORY Rue traces its name to the Greek word *ruta*, meaning repentance. It has long been a symbol of sorrow and repentance and was called "herb of grace", after the god-given grace that usually follows true repentance. Greeks used it to combat the nervousness they experienced when they had to eat with foreigners who were often suspected of having evil powers. In Rome they used it to improve eyesight.

MAGICAL PROPERTIES AND USES There is a lot in a name, and that is particularly true for rue. This herb's strongest power, in fact, is to bring momentous awareness of one's own mistake to the people who are subject to her magical influence. That might mean that you

would want to use it for yourself, to discover where you went wrong, or for others, to see if anything fishy is going on. This might apply to purely practical mistakes or to deeper misunderstandings and misgivings.

For example you are working on a project, might it be a business plan, a creative piece, or the reorganization of an office, and you just can't come to grips with it. Use rue, and immediately you will see what you were doing wrong: what you overlooked, where the hidden door was.

Or maybe you are emotionally involved with someone; you know that something is not quite right but cannot put your finger on it. Use rue, and you will have a flash of understanding as to exactly what the problem is: whether you may have unrealistic expectations about that person or whether that person is actually trying to deceive you in some way or whatever the problem might be.

Use this herb by putting a cupful of it dried into a bowl. Prepare yourself for magic. Call the power air and raising the bowl with both your hands over the symbol of the element, ask it to reveal the truth to you. Use simple words which express for you the core of the situation you want to better understand.

Laurel ranges in size anywhere from a medium bush to a large tree. The leaves can easily be found in any vegetable market; dry them in a heated place and keep in glass jars.

The answer will come to you in the form of a dream or an intuition. Keep the bowl with the rue next to you until you have the answer. Be careful, though, that nobody touches or eats it, as it can be dangerous.

LAUREL (BAY)
Laurus nobilus

This is a plant which can grow from a medium bush to a big tree. Gather the fresh leaves from trees, or buy them: you can find fresh laurel leaves in most vegetable markets. You can dry them in a heated place and keep them in glass jars.

MEDICINAL PROPERTIES   The parts of this plant used medicinally are the leaves and the fruits. It favors digestion. It is slightly tonic and purifying. Applied externally it is a deodorant and soothing. In the bath water it makes a relaxing bath. Bay oil pressed from the berries and leaves can be used in salves and liniments for rheumatism, bruises and skin problems.

NAME AND HISTORY   The name *laurus* derives from Celtic *lawr*, verdant, for its characteristic of evergreen, and *nobilis* because it was used to crown heroes and poets. In Greek and Roman mythology the nymph Daphne was changed at her own wish into a laurel tree by her father to keep her from being attacked by Apollo. Apollo made the tree sacred and declared that he would wear a crown of its leaves, as would men who return victorious from the war.

Laurel was also given to poets, statesmen, athletes and anybody who would distinguish himself in a worthy deed.

MAGICAL PROPERTIES AND USES   This is the herb of glory and fame, as simple as that. Use laurel in an incantation and you will immediately see the ways to put yourself in the course of immortality (symbolically speaking). Keep laurel next to you, on your desk, in your dressing room, in the locker room on an important occasion, and you will be sure to succeed.

Laurel is used by keeping the leaves intact,

The prickling thorn and the beautiful flower exist together on the hawthorn bush — the Latin name derives from hardness and sharpness but the original use was always associated with sweet hope, marriage and offspring.

possibly fresh (but lacking those, dry ones will do), and placing them on your heart, your head, your feet, your hands or wherever the glory will spring from. So if you are a writer or a poet it will be on your head. If you are an artist on your hands. If you want glory as a model you will place them on your body, etc.

You are to sit or lie so inside your circle, if you have one, or just in front of the four elements and call the power air. Address it so:

"I invoke you air, and with the help of ancient laurel, open my eyes to the ways of glory" (or heart or mind or whatever).

HAWTHORN
Crataegus oxyacantha

This is a bush with prickly thorns and lovely white flowers. It can become a tree when it is allowed to grow. If there are hawthorn bushes around you, gather the flowers at the beginning of flowering time, that is April-May. Otherwise buy the dry flowers in a herb shop, and keep them in paper or linen bags.

MEDICINAL PROPERTIES Hawthorn normalizes the blood pressure by regulating heart action. Extended use will usually lower blood pressure. It is good for heart muscle weakened

by age. It is also good for nervous conditions and insomnia. A decoction of flowers and leaves is astringent and tonic, specific for greasy and impure skin. Makes a relaxing bath.

NAME AND HISTORY *Crataegus* comes from the Greek *krathos*, strength, because of the hardness of the wood. *Oxyacantha* comes from the Greek *oxys*, pointed, and *acanda*, thorn. In spite of the prickly thorns in ancient Greece and Rome the hawthorn had happy associations, being linked with sweet hope, marriage and children. Dedicated to Hymen, the god of marriage, the hawthorn was used as symbol of

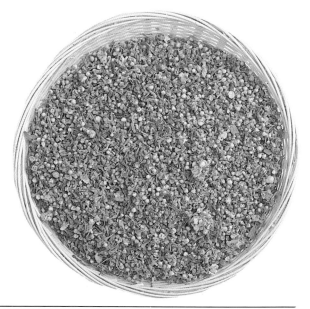

hope at weddings in Greece. The Romans put hawthorn leaves in the cradles of newborn babies to ward off evil spirits.

In Medieval Europe hawthorn had an entirely different image. Regarded as an unlucky plant, it was thought that bringing its branches inside would portend the death of one of the household members. Witches were suspected to turn themselves into Hawthorn bushes on Walpurgis Night.

MAGICAL PROPERTIES AND USES This is the herb of happy life, in work and in family. As that covers a great deal of human interests, you can see why hawthorn has always had such a great reputation as a magic plant. Keep a hawthorn sprig in your place of work and at home, and your happiness is safeguarded. Drink a hawthorn infusion during magic incantations and you will see ways of keeping the happiness of your family and your work.

HERBS CHART

Remember that when you create your own herb magic, follow the example given and always pay attention to the way the herbs are used medicinally. You should never, by any means, make a potion out of a poisonous herb, or bathe in an irritating one.

The way the herb can be used magically — by drinking an infusion of it, by burning it, by keeping it somewhere, by sprinkling it in the wind — does not alone constitute the whole magic. You need to follow the procedure of calling the powers, check with the suggestions of various different methods of magic corresponding to the element and fit your herb into that. However, the suggestions in the last column can be used as quick magic hints, when you do not have the time to go through the whole process.

HERB	ENGLISH NAME	LATIN NAME	MEDICINAL PROPERTIES
	ANGELICA	*Angelica archangelica*	Appetizer, digestive, tonic, antispasmodic. In little doses it is tonic, in large depressant.
	ANISE	*Pimpinella anisum*	Digestive, stimulant, tonic, sedative in case of insomnia and nervousness.
	BALM	*Melissa officinalis*	Digestive, sedative, useful for female complaints and nervous problems, purifier and decongestant of the skin
	BASIL	*Ocimum basilicum*	Appetizer, aromatic, tonic, anti-inflammatory, antiseptic, antispasmodic.
	BURDOCK	*Arctium lappa*	Diuretic, purgative, antiseptic.
	CAMOMILE	*Matricaria chamomilla*	Digestive, sedative, anti-inflammatory for the skin, make good wash for open sores, wounds and eyes.
	ELECAMPANE	*Inula helenium*	For treatments of the liver and kidneys, for respiratory system, as a wash for skin problems like itching, eczem herpes.
	FOXGLOVE	*Digitalis purpurea*	Narcotic, sedative, cardiac. POISONOUS – use under medical supervision. Touchi the plant with bare skin might cause nausea, headaches and rashes.

PART(S) TO USE	MAGICAL PROPERTIES	MAGICAL USE
Roots and fruits	This herb brings on the gift of temperance.	Elixir: see detailed herb.
Fruits (improperly called seeds)	The aroma of the fruit of this herb has the power of awakening subtle energies needed for magic.	Put fruits in linen cloth, for magic clothes.
Flowery tops and leaves	Soothes away hurts and fears in magic related to love pains.	Infusion: 0,5g in 100g water. Drink during incantation.
Flowery tops and leaves	Since ancient times basil is known for its magical property of bringing wealth.	Powdered basil for wealth and prosperity. Sprinkle on person.
Root and leaves	For cleansing magic when feeling bad, highly negative about oneself or others.	Root decoction: 100g in 1l of water. Apply on the face. On rinsing pronounce magic words of purification.
Flowers	Prepares mind and body for magic operations. Brings peace.	Infusion: 4g in 100ml of water. Drink during magic preparations.
Rhyzome	Has the property of dispelling violent, angry vibrations.	Hide a sachet of dried herb in the room.
Leaves	This herb has the power of opening the one who uses it magically to strong sexual love.	Put powder in box. Place close to you. DO NOT ABSORB – POISON!

HERB	ENGLISH NAME	LATIN NAME	MEDICINAL PROPERTIES
	GARLIC	*Allium sativum*	Digestive, antiseptic, purifier.
	HAWTHORN	*Crataegus oxyacantha*	Normalizes blood pressure, regulates the skin.
	HELLEBORE	*Helleborus niger*	Stimulates the heart, treats depression and skin problems. POISONOUS – use only under medical supervision. Contact with the bruised herb may cause dermatitis.
	HENBANE	*Hyoscyamus niger*	Sedative, narcotic, used in oil for earache and rheumatism. POISONOUS – use only under medical supervision.
	JIMSON WEED	*Datura stramonium*	Hypnotic, narcotic, in a tincture against coughing and asthma. POISONOUS – use only under medical supervision.
	LAUREL	*Laurus nobilis*	Aromatic, favors digestion, tonic, purifying, soothing.
	MALLOW	*Malva sylvestris*	Treats inflammations and irritations of respiratory passages. Against swelled eyes.
	MANDRAKE	*European: Mandragora officinarum*	Hay fever, asthma, cough. POISONOUS – use only under medical supervision.

PART(S) TO USE	MAGICAL PROPERTIES	MAGICAL USE
Bulb	Protective charm. Keeps you strong. Brings togetherness to the family.	Hang in kitchen, patio, windowsill.
Flowers and fruits	It brings success and happiness in all working matters.	Infusion: 1g in 100ml water. Drink during incantation.
Rootstock	This herb's influence opens you to the mysteries of different realms of existence. Use together with vervain when attempting to reach other worldly beings.	Gather the fresh herb (December) and place it on your left when needed. DO NOT ABSORB – POISON!
Whole plant	Improves faculties of clairvoyance and divination.	Burn a pinch of the herb in the burner, after having called the power fire. DO NOT INHALE VAPORS, DO NOT ABSORB – POISON!
Seeds and leaves	Releases inhibitions. Call the power fire, and burn this herb to have a glimpse of what your deep wishes and desires are.	Burn throwing pinches of it in burner. DO NOT ABSORB – POISON!
Leaves and fruit	It opens you to the possibility of great fame and victory in your activities.	Call the power air and place garland over your head.
Flowers and leaves	Softens your character. For a girl – makes her softer and more feminine. For a man – makes him appreciate small pleasures and beauty in life.	Make a decoction of flowers and leaves. Add to bath.
Rootstock	Mystic plant. Strong luck charm for fertility and protection.	As amulet. DO NOT ABSORB – POISON!

HERB	ENGLISH NAME	LATIN NAME	MEDICINAL PROPERTIES
	MARJORAM	*Origanum majorana*	Aromatic, digestive, sedative for headaches and cramps.
	MINT	*Mentha piperita*	Tonic, for nervousness and nerve related problems, cram
	MONKSHOOD	*Aconitum napellus*	For pains of neuralgia, sciatica, rheumatism, chronic skin problems. POISONOUS – use only under medical supervision. Sm doses can cause death.
	MUGWORT	*Artemisia vulgaris*	Appetizer, digestive, sedative.
	NETTLE	*Urtica dioica*	Diuretic, purifying, anti-inflammatory of the digestive system.
	NIGHTSHADE	*Solanum nigrum*	Purgative, narcotic, used against skin problems, tumors, fever and pain. POISONOUS – use only under medical supervision.
	PARSLEY	*Petroselinum sativum*	Appetizer, expectorant, diuretic, regularizes menstrual cycle
	ROSEMARY	*Rosmarinus officinalis*	Antiseptic, antispasmodic, stimulant, good for hair.

PART(S) TO USE	MAGICAL PROPERTIES	MAGICAL USE
Flowery tops	As in ancient times, this herb accompanies the dead in their travels to the other worlds. Also helps you accept profound changes in your life.	Burn over burner when someone or something dies, physically or figuratively.
Flowery tops and leaves	Takes excessive heat off emotions and/or situations.	Infusion: 1-2g in 100ml of water for drinking.
Rootstock and leaves	Chases pain, both physical and emotional.	Burn the herb on your burner and sprinkle ashes in the wind in nature. DO NOT ABSORB – POISON!
Rootstock and leaves	This is the traveler's herb. Protects safe and happy travel and holiday.	Put in a sachet and take with you.
Top part of plant	Resolves uncomfortable, "prickly" situations: petty jealousies, envy, slanderous gossip, etc.	Infusion: 50g of flowers in 1l of boiling water, steep for 10 minutes, and sprinkle on room and people involved.
Leaves	Frees your energy, helps you to find out what you really want to do.	Wait for a west wind to blow and call air, disperse a pinch of the dry powdered herb in the wind. DO NOT ABSORB – POISON!
Seeds and leaves	Good for incantations related to physical well-being, restores health, strength and vitality.	Call the power earth and drink an infusion of it. Can also be used in conjunction with other drinkable herbs.
Small branches and leaves	This very happy herb brings contentment and love.	See detailed herb.

HERB	ENGLISH NAME	LATIN NAME	MEDICINAL PROPERTIES
	RUE	*Ruta graveolens*	To cure palpitations in menopause, provokes uterine contractions. Overdose can be mildly poisonous.
	SAGE	*Salvia officinalis*	Anti-inflammatory, astringent, balsam, antiseptic.
	SKULLCAP	*Scutellaria lateriflora*	Good for spasms, convulsions, restlessness, brings on menstruation.
	THYME	*Thymus vulgaris*	Expectorant, antiseptic, tonic, for gastritis and lack of appetite, a mouthwash.
	VALERIAN	*Valeriana officinalis*	Calming, hypnotic, sedative of the nervous system, anti-neuralgic.
	VERVAIN	*Verbena officinalis*	Astringent, diuretic, digestive, purifying.
	WITCH HAZEL	*Hamamelis virginiana*	Decongestant of the genital apparatus, refreshing and decongesting the skin.
	WORMWOOD	*Artemisia absinthium*	Stimulates vitality, appetite, liver and gallbladder.

PART(S) TO USE	MAGICAL PROPERTIES	MAGICAL USE
Top part of plant	This herb of repentance helps people see their mistakes – yours and others!	Hang dry indoors, from ceiling, doorsteps, etc. where it is not very visible.
Leaves	Brings health and beauty. Always good for all-around improvement magic.	Infusion: 1g in 100ml water.
Whole plant	To relax before an important occasion.	Infusion: 5g in 100g of water. Steep 30 min. Use in incantations.
Leaves	Inspires courage and strength. Use before difficult situations.	Throw a handful of herb with its flowers in the bath water.
Rootstock	For dream magic and for reconciliation magic.	See detailed herb.
Whole plant	Druids used it as magic plant for incantations. Use for opening to a new love.	Infusion: 5g in 100ml of water.
Leaves	Brings charm and attractiveness. Makes you irresistible.	Throw a handful of leaves in the bath water.
Flowery tops and leaves	Vitality tonic, for after magic sessions.	Infusion: 5g in 100ml of water. Use in incantations.

The Magic of Flowers

If you love flowers, if while walking down country lanes you find yourself stopping and staring at those little creatures of light and color, if you have been standing over them in wonder, feeling that there must be more to flowers than just the pleasure they give to your sight and smell — then flower magic is for you, and you should choose them as a primary tool.

Doing magic with flowers is both very easy and extremely difficult since there are no hard and fast rules to go by. Contrary to herbs, which have a strong identity of their own and work pretty much in the same way regardless of who is using them, flowers react strongly to outside factors when doing magic. Herbs work best on the physical plane and through a more or less direct interaction with the body; flowers act on the emotions, and their magic moves through feelings.

It is a precise and delightful task learning to know one's own flowers. It means choosing them, watching them, smelling them, having them close by for a length of time, and noticing one's own reactions to that flower's closeness. If a cornflower will always work for me in a fertility philter, it might not do so for you. Therefore working with flowers is a very creative exercise, where you will have to get to know each species and what its use is.

Here it is important to note that some plants can be used in magic either as flowers or as herbs. If you use a plant as an herb, you will use those specific properties which you are freeing by drinking it or burning it, or whatever method you choose. Those properties would be the same for anyone who would use that plant in that way. If you use that same plant for flower magic, you will use it through your heart, in the way its energy reacts to your own energy. That reaction might mean cleanliness to some or devotion to others.

Plants which can double up in magic as herbs and as flowers are those which have an important flowering and also strong medicinal properties and are normally used in more ways than as decoration. Lavender is one such plant. Another one is heather and there are many more.

If you happen to have a garden where you grow your favorite flowers, there is of course nothing better than using those flowers for your magic. Otherwise, choose the flowers which are fresh in season at the moment: you can find them in shops or flower markets or can gather them in the countryside.

Some people feel there is something sad about a cut flower because it has been taken away from its environment and it will soon die. They think that the true beauty of a flower can only be seen when it stands free and natural in its home ground. This is true. But it is also true and important that flowers do have a magic potential, which most often remains untouched, and that they are happy to be able to fulfill it. A red rose in an alcove, looking over the joys of two lovers, is part of the magic of that moment; she has helped it to come into existence. She is no more just a flower, but a presence in her own right.

When a certain flower is not available fresh (and that is often bound to be the case), do not entirely rely on its dried petals and leaves. While using dry herbs works very well in herb magic, it does not have the same effect in flower magic. The spirit of the flower leaves it when it dies. A dry flower carries the memory of what it once was, but not much of the active magical properties.

You need to also use its essence, its perfume. A flower carries much of its magic in its scent. Using that you will be able to find its presence and its magic.

TO KNOW A FLOWER

Here are a few points to follow if you want to get familiar with flower magic.

Find a beautiful, well decorated note-book in which you can collect your information on the particular flowers, your impressions, your feelings.

Look around and find the flower which at this moment attracts you most, not necessarily the one you like best, but the one you feel most interested in.

Gather as many of that flower as you can. If you can fill up your home with it, all the better. At least fill one room (best of all your own magic place) while you are studying it. If it is impractical for you to do this, one specimen at least should stay in your magic place for at least three days. In order to become close to the flower during the next three days find the time for one hour each day to sit silently by them.

Be open to it, breathe in its scent. Even the most odorless flower has a scent of some kind. Stay away from the man-made corruption of some species, which have lost all of the original perfume of the flower. Many modern varieties of rose are scentless. That is just a crime.

Look at the flower, noticing all the details, but most of all be receptive to the emotions and feelings that the flower will evoke in you. If you find some memories and old tales surfacing in your mind pay attention to this, as it might be important to the function that the flower will draw for you. Write down everything

under the heading you will have made on that flower's name. Write it down beginning with your first reaction, your first thoughts, and then every day try to feel deeper and deeper what that flower has to say to you. It might be that a particular flower, after a first moment of excitement, leaves you rather cold. Don't force things. It might be that this flower's magic just isn't for you. Don't worry, there are many other paths to choose from!

Also gather some information from a good botanical book on the origin of the flower, its flowering times, if pharmaceutical uses and cosmetic uses for that flower are known. Look up any legend and lore about that flower and write down the things that capture your attention. Be sure to do this last, as you don't want to influence your own perception of the relationship between you and the flower.

After you have done all this, you can start seeing how you can use it in magic. In that too, let your intuition guide you. If a flower gives you a strong feeling of plenty, perhaps it could be used in a fertility spell or incantation — or it could be used in conjunction with other herbs

in a philter. Hereafter are shown examples of how to use some flowers in magic. This, if you choose, can be a starting place for your own experiences.

Write down your own experiments and their success or failures. Never do more than one incantation at a time. That is true for any kind of magic. What follows is an indication and an example. Be sure to find out your own true relationship to the particular flowers.

It is very possible that some flowers will mean the same thing to different people. Maybe you are acquainted with the "collective unconscious" notion. If it is true that we react individually to each different flower and they to us, it is also true that beside the superficial conscious mind that determines our differences, a universal, collective unconscious mind exists, where all basic symbols spring from and our separate identities disappear. If you meet with a flower at that level it is very possible that you will find the same meaning in it that thousands of others have done before. But it must be a spontaneous happening, something that first you find for yourself and then look around and see that others, too, have been there. And always remember, there are no hard and fast rules in this game. What feels right is right, and what really works is right.

The Latin name for water lily means virgin — given by the Greeks who wished to mirror the aloofness of this beautiful flower.

METHODS OF FLOWER MAGIC

Here we shall explain some of the methods which you can use to do magic with your flowers:

BY AIR   Write a spell and keep it under the flower's vase, until it has blossomed; or keep the flower by your bedside, and as you fall asleep, ask its spirit to show you an answer to your query, a way out of a situation.

BY FIRE   Burn the essence of the flower; or let a candle burn continuously until the blossom you have placed next to it is open.

BY WATER   Let the flower's petals steep in a glass of well water, under the full moon, for a whole night. Drink the water during the Calling the Powers ritual.

BY EARTH   Plant a seed in a little pot, giving it the desire, or purpose you want it to accomplish. When the plant is ready the wish is granted.

Some flowers you might use for magic are:

WATER LILY
Nymphaea

The name *nymphaea* comes from the Greek *nymphe* which means virgin. The Greeks gave this name to the plant because of the beautiful

aloofness of it, which in our day makes it a flower of unique beauty.

The various species of the *nymphaea* are found all over the world, and ancient civilizations praised their beauty. In ancient Egypt the lotus flower was represented on the tombs and monuments, and in India the lotus has always been a religious symbol, where the ultimate state of meditation, samadhi, is represented by the lotus flower.

In the literature of many countries the *nymphaea* comes to represent a thing of grace and purity and of virginal beauty; like the spirit which springs forth from the chaos, the beautiful flower floats on mud.

MAGICAL USES Water lilies have sedative powers when applied to the heart. Contemplating the purity of the flower, untouched by the surrounding, the heart again finds its very own core of grace. When you feel that life is just too much to bear, go to a pond and let the spirit of the water lilies soothe your troubles. It is like a mellow blanket of white and dew descending in your mind, cooling all heat, rounding all edges, taking the sharpness away from pain, until you sleep, or cry, and smile again.

The water lily is wonderful in all kinds of love magic. If love is the cause of pain, no matter what the reason is, the water lily will help you find again that place in your heart which is virgin and unaffected, that part that remains pure and whole throughout all of life's difficulties.

Since it may not be easy to find a water lily when you need one, unless you have a pond in your garden, use the essence of it for your incantation. As you sit and complete yourself in the circle, dab a few drops of the perfume on your wrists and inhale the scent. Conjure the image of the flower and see yourself sitting by a pond, in a green forest. Feel the dew on the ground, and hear the noises of the undergrowth. See the flower floating simply on the water and see yourself as that flower. You can imagine yourself curled up inside it, floating weightlessly above the waters.

You should perform this magic in the evenings, before going to sleep. Then, leave your magic place, without performing any of your usual nightly activities (you should have performed those before starting the magic), go straight to bed and let yourself go to sleep, while you are still "inside the bud". When you wake in the morning you will feel very different. Your problems might still be there, but they will be further removed from you, at a distance from which it will be easier to find a solution. If that night you have a dream which

The Christians tell us in their legends that the daisies were the tears of Mary — the Greeks dedicated the flower to Aphrodite. Always a love flower, we all know that its petals will predict whether we are loved or not.

you remember well, pay particular attention to it, for it will be the spirit of the *nymphaea* helping you.

PRACTICAL INFORMATION   The water lily is commonly found in ponds and slow streams. The flower and rootstock are used as sedatives.

To keep, shake the water off the flowers and make them into strings of flowers which you will hang in a well aired, shadowy place. Cut the rootstock into slices and dry them in the sun. Keep in glass or porcelain jars.

Be careful: when the flower is scentless, it is probably not a pond lily, but a different variety of the plant, which would not produce the same effect in magic.

DAISY
Bellis perennis

Opinions differ around the origin of the name *bellis*. Some think it derives from the name of the daughters of King Danao, some from the Latin word *bellum* which means war, because apparently daisies were used to cure wounds. Another, perhaps more credible version, believes that it comes from the Latin word *bellus* which means beautiful.

The name daisy, instead, comes from the Anglo-Saxon *daeges eage* which means day's eye because the flowers open their petals in the daytime and close them at night.

The daisy is very old in mankind's history. In the Christian legend the daisies were the tears of Mary, and in ancient Greece they were dedicated to Aphrodite. The daisy has always been used as a love oracle, whereby the little petals are taken off one by one, reciting "he loves me, he loves me not." In Germany daisies picked between twelve and one p.m. have magical qualities.

MAGICAL USES   Daisies are everywhere in the spring. They are the most common flower to be found and children will play interminably with them making chains, games and so on. They carry the magic of ordinariness, of every-

The other most favorite use of the daisy is employed by young children who will happily make daisy chains for a whole picnic outing — the love aspect of this flower extends to all ages.

---

day life. They bring the feelings of simplicity, clarity, playfulness.

It is good to use the daisy when stress has covered up the capacity to enjoy simple, everyday actions. When you are in the middle of a working crisis, or when you have been working too much, and you are so stressed and overtired that you just can't find the simplicity of your own heart anymore, try this: on your way home from work stop at the florist and buy a bunch of daisies. As soon as you arrive home put them in a vase with abundant water.

When all evening activities are over, prepare yourself for magic and place the flowers in front of you, together with the symbols of the elements. Let your eyes rest on the daisies and relax; just looking at the flowers let your mind be empty. While you breathe in and out, imagine the essence of the flower coming inside you with the in-breath and the stress leaving you with the out-breath.

Call the powers, as explained in the beginning ritual of part one. According to the element answering you, you will use the daisy in the appropriate magic.

Let us say that the element which answers is air. From the magic of the four elements, you are acquainted with some of these methods of magic. For the element air, you choose to

Lavandula means to wash; washing away fears and
purifying. New brides to be would adorn themselves
with lavender before the first night of marriage to
soothe their fears.

operate a spell. On a clean, white paper, write a
few words:

Through the daisy's power
a simple spell is done.
In the work I succeed
it is harm to none.

Place the folded-up spell under the vase and
leave it next to your bedside for three nights.
On the morning of the third night, all your
problems will have disappeared. You will go to
work with fresh and renewed energies, and you
will again be able to enjoy all the little things
which make life worthy of living.

PRACTICAL INFORMATION The daisy is
commonly found anywhere from the seaside to
the mountains in fields and pastures. It is also
widely cultivated as an ornamental plant. It
blooms from March to September.

Parts used medicinally are flowers and leaves. They are taken at the beginning of flowering
time, in March. They are put to dry in a well-
aired place, in the shade and then kept in a
container of glass or porcelain. They can work
as expectorant, laxative, purgative, tonic. They

help heal inflamed swellings and burns. The
juice can be used externally for injuries and
suppuration.

LAVENDER
Lavandula vera or *officinalis*

The name *lavandula* comes from the Latin
lavare, meaning to wash and referring to the use
of the flower in bath water for scenting. In
ancient Rome lavender was dedicated to the
goddess Vesta, and her sacred virgins, the
vestals, adorned their hair with it during the
ceremonies.

From this virginal tradition of the plant, the
custom of scenting brides' beds and clothes
with lavender has remained, so that lavender
can soothe their fears in the first night of
marriage.

Lavender is also said to be one of the herbs
which witches used to throw in the fire at
midsummer night, as offering to their Gods.

MAGICAL USES Lavender works for freshness and cleanliness and with the feelings of
honesty and directness. It has many uses in
magic, both as herb and as a flower. As a
flower, lavender is miraculous when used in
cases of unresolved guilt. This is the case when
you find that in your emotional connection

The smell of fresh lavender is entirely different from the smell that is found in the lavender cushions purchased in stores — if you have never smelled the fresh flower you have missed a most important experience.

with the world there is always a feeling of it "not being quite right". When no matter what confirmations of love you receive from people and situations, you always feel somewhere ill at ease. The guilt is blackening your perception of yourself and of the world.

It might be that a particular event precipitates the awareness of this situation. Perhaps you have just obtained a break-through in your career — you should be happy; it was what you had been struggling for for a long time, but still you feel uncomfortable. Perhaps you have just met a splendid person who seems to be very well inclined towards you, and you, even recognizing the good intentions of that person, can't shake off the feeling of suspicion.

This is a very good opportunity to use lavender. Lavender will reach your heart and act on it directly, in the emotional sphere, washing away all dark shadows.

The flowers bloom in summer; you should find a field of lavender, cut a big bunch and prepare this magic oil from them which you will be able to use when the need arises.

Cut the flowers during a full moon night. Take the flowers home, and in the morning prepare the oil by putting a generous handful of the fresh flowers and half a liter of olive oil into a glass jar. Put the jar under the sun and leave it for a few days. Under the jar you will write this spell:

By the virtue of lavender
and the virtue of the sun,
as the moon goes, so will my sins.

Filter the liquid and put it away in an hermetically sealed bottle, until you need it.

PRACTICAL INFORMATION Lavender grows on stony and gravelly grounds. It is widely cultivated and often wild. It flowers from July to September.

Parts used medicinally are the flowers. They are gathered at the beginning of flowering time, in June-July. They are put to dry in bunches in the shade; when they are well dried the flowers are separated from the rest of the plant. They are kept in glass containers away from the light.

There are many uses for this lovely plant.

Taken externally the flowers purify the skin and stimulate the superficial circulation, particularly the scalp's. It is also useful in purifying the breath and the mouth. A handful of flowers in the bath water makes it tonic and purifying. Internally lavender is diuretic, stimulant, tonic, sedative. Good for headache, fainting and dizziness.

The white lily flowers in May or June and originates in lower Asia, though now may be found cultivated all over Europe. Its petals and bulbs are used in many herbal cures for burns and inflammations of the skin.

WHITE LILY
Lilium cancucum

An origin of the word *lilium* can be found in the Hebrew name Susan (*Schuschan*), which means purity but also lily. Since those times come the associations of the lily with purity and virtue. In the Bible it is often used as a symbol of comparison for virtue — "pure as the lily". The lily was also one of the ornaments of the temple of Solomon.

Back in time, though, in ancient Greece, a more earthy meaning was given to the flower. Lily was the flower dedicated to Hera, the goddess mother of the sky. The legend says that Hercules, suckling the milk from Hera, was so forceful that he spilled great quantities of it everywhere. Some drops also fell on Earth, and from those grew the first lilies.

Certainly this flower is one of the oldest on Earth, perhaps a survivor of the Ice Age.

Edward Bach, co-author of *The Bach Flower Remedies*, advises the use of it to help in cases when the feeling of separateness is too strong for well-being.

In the past century, when people re-discovered the pleasure of giving messages with flowers, giving a white lily to a girl meant feeling respect for her purity. (If you are hopefully cultivating some handsome man and he presents you with a white lily, you know you have to let him know that he can go ahead!)

MAGICAL USES　The white lily symbolizes the spiritual life, the beauty of those rarefied moments when it is possible to view all life from a core of beauty and purity, from where it is possible to see all good and bad as pure love.

Keep it around you when you feel the need to elevate yourself over the ties and worries of everyday life. Use its incantations to purify a love affair when you feel that too much anger, jealousy and misunderstandings are clouding what otherwise are good gentle feelings (but you must be clear about the truth of this love — if there was nothing to begin with, no lily can give it back to you).

Use when you want to open your heart to new values and meanings. Perhaps you have just ended a relationship, and you feel that next time it should be very different. Your heart is ready for something new. This magic lends itself very well to being performed in conjunction with Stone magic. A ruby would be perfect.

The white lily can also represent the soul of an unborn child. Planting one in earth is a good way of calling him or her.

PRACTICAL INFORMATION　This beautiful

white flower is originally from lower Asia but is now widely cultivated all over Europe and America. Its flowering time is May to June.

The lily petals and bulbs are used in herbal medicine. The petals are to be collected at the opening of the flowers in May-June. The bulbs are taken when the plant is resting, that is from August to September. The petals are to be dried in the shade or in a moderate oven, then conserved in containers of glass or porcelain. The bulbs are to be peeled like an onion and the layers of skin are dried in the sun and kept as the petals.

For burns and inflammations of the skin, the bulbs can be cooked and applied to the affected part. The extract of the bulb is also good for improving the tone and elasticity of old and relaxed skin.

CORNFLOWER
Centaurea cyanus

Its genus name, *Centaurea cyanus*, derives from the mythic Centaurus, teacher of Achilles, who, having hurt his foot, cured it with the juice of this flower. Another legend says that Cyanus

was in love with the divine Flora. One day he was found dead in a field next to this flower. From that day the Goddess ordered that the beautiful blue flowers should take the name of her beloved.

MAGICAL USES It grows in the cornfields, in the abundance of the golden harvest. Summer sees its blue eyes shine between the ripe corn. Cornflower is love-in-abundance, abundance inside and out, and therefore fertility. Gathering cornflower and having it around, imparts a feeling of abundance and plenty, and makes you experience the world as a rich and generous place.

Use cornflower in two cases: the obvious one is in fertility matters, the other when the capacity of feeling the richness of existence is impaired and the person feels poor, like a beggar in a mean environment. The influence of the cornflower in this case will be to re-

Pages 138, 139 and left
**The Latin name of the cornflower derives from
ancient legends of love and natural cure and the
summer harvest in the cornfields will see the flower's
blue eye shining in the sun.**

establish the feeling of plenty, and the joy of it.
It lends itself well to combinations with other
flowers and herbs.

PRACTICAL INFORMATION It is an annual
herb native to Europe but also found cultivated
in the USA. It is found in fields and gravels but
most often in cornfields which have not been
weeded chemically. Cornflower flowers from
May to June.

Cornflower does not have great medicinal
properties. The capitulum can be used as a
tonic and a diuretic and also as eyewash. A
handful of flowers in the bath water is excellent
for delicate skins.

Gather the capitulums during flowering time
and put them to dry in a shady, well aired
place. Keep in glass or porcelain containers,
away from the light.

SUNFLOWER
Helianthus annuus

Helianthus comes from the Greek word *elios*,
sun and *anthos*, flower; that is "flower of the
sun". *Annuus* means annual.

In Europe the sunflower was grown for the
first time in 1562, in the royal garden of
Madrid, from seeds imported from Peru and
Mexico, where Atahualpa, the King God of the

Incas had as his symbol a solid gold sunflower. In fact, the Incas believed the sunflower to have magical properties because of its geometrical perfection.

The world famous Bach Flower Remedies advises the use of the sunflower for balancing out the ego and restoring self-esteem.

MAGICAL USES This flower is definitely worth some study. Its dimensions, its behavior (it follows the sun during the course of the day) and its history, make it quite impressive.

You should learn to respect its strength, and to use it carefully in magic. Its energy is strong, vital and male. It issues courage and action. Use them to give added strength to an incantation (if it is an active, expanding one). If you are a woman they are also very appropriate in invoking the presence of a man into your life — if you want a very strong one!

Sunflower is also good to use when one's self image is somewhat distorted in reflecting a person who is feeble and unable to take on any of life's trials. For example, you are faced with a situation which is particularly taxing. Maybe you have lost your job and are alone to support your children. Certainly it is not easy, but if you just collapse and whine to all your friends and relatives, and do nothing positive, the situation will only drag on endlessly. You need

to unsheathe all your reserves of strength and will-power, tell yourself that you will succeed and think of nothing else. If you have a voice inside which repeats "I will never make it", you are not going to go far. In this case do a sunflower magic.

If you can, wait for a south wind to raise. Prepare yourself for magic and call the powers. You will have a few dry petals of the sunflower ready (if you can have a fresh flower, so much the better). Call the power fire and throw the petals into the fire. As they burn, with your imagination, see the flames start at your toes and work their way up through your legs to your belly and chest. Feel how they are warming your body up and, by freeing it from fear, they are releasing strength and determination. The flames rise through to your head, and leave from the top of your head. They leave your mind clear and set. You will know how to face the task at hand, taking one thing at a time, without letting your mind wander on the possible downfalls.

PRACTICAL INFORMATION Originally from Peru, sunflower was introduced in Europe around 1600. It is now widely cultivated for its seed production but also for its use as an ornamental plant. Its seeds and flowery tops are also used medicinally. The tops are obtained in

The geometrical perfection of the sunflower gave the ancient Incas the belief that it contained great magical powers and today it is capable of re-balancing the ego and restoring the self-esteem.

August-September, gathering the lateral capitulums. The big central capitulums are cut in October, at ripening time. The seeds are then shelled out of them. The flowery tops are hung to dry in the shade in a well aired place; the seeds are laid out in a dry place. Both are then kept in bags of paper or linen. The seeds are good for nervous conditions and headaches and colds. The tops are diuretic and aid the digestion.

SWEET VIOLET
Viola odorata

The sweet violet was one of the flowers which Proserpina was gathering when she was taken by Pluto. And it was also the favorite food of Io, transformed by Jupiter from nymph into heifer.

In Athens violets were used to embellish homes and temples, and the Romans used it in enormous amounts to decorate banquets since they believed that violets had the power to defend them against drunkenness.

In Athens it was customary to cover the dead with violets to symbolize the beauty and the fragility of life. In Rome violets were put on the graves of children, as a symbol of purity and modesty.

Pages 146 and 147
Sweet violet, symbol of spiritual understanding is a modest, vulnerable and shy flower that will make your surroundings vibrate with sweetness.

Shakespeare also loves the violet: Oberon knows that the juice of the violet petals rubbed on the eyes of a sleeping person will make him or her fall in love with the first one that they will see on waking.

MAGICAL USES Hiding her graces in the tall leaves by a pond, under a tree, violet is so tender and soft smelling. Having violets around makes the house vibrate with the sweetest vibrations. She is shy, modest, vulnerable. Her color, violet, is the symbol of spirituality.

As the sunflower represents the male principle in flower magic, so the violet represents the female. When the feelings of shyness and vulnerability become a problem, the violet can show you the beauty and preciousness of those feelings.

Unfortunately in modern society, being vulnerable is regarded as a negative attribute; the image of the cool, tough man or woman is regarded as the most attractive. And if you are sitting at home crying while your girl-friend is making a collection of devastating suitors, you are very probably going to join the crowd and think that being vulnerable is *out* and that not caring is best!

Well, before you are too far along on that path, go out and buy a bunch of violets (better still a little pot full), take your good magic

book, and do a little magic. Violets will show you that being vulnerable is *in*, and that being tough is good for the farmyard, but not for things of the heart.

Violet magic can bring you into the space where you can see that the same energy which might be making you suffer now is that which makes you appreciate the softness and the beauty of the world and which makes you share it with others. Violets will show you that being able to feel that way is a quality, not a failing. And that the reason you perhaps feel hurt sometimes is only that you think of it as being a failing.

PRACTICAL INFORMATION   Sweet violet is a small European plant that is commonly cultivated and also grows wild in meadows, thickets, hedges and along roadsides and the edges of woods. Flowering time is March to May.

A few drops of jasmine oil on the body, mixed with almond oil will overcome any frigidity and if you dream of jasmine it can mean good luck in love.

The rootstock and flowers of this plant are also used medicinally. Garden violet is primarily a herb for respiratory problems. A tea made from the leaves is a soothing gargle and relieves headaches. It is also used as a calming agent for insomnia and hysterical or nervous problems. The rootstock is collected in spring or autumn; the flowers, as soon as they come out in March. Dry the rootstock in the sun and keep it in bags of paper or linen. The flowers are dried in the dark, in a warm and well-aired place. Keep them then in glass or porcelain containers.

JASMINE
Jasminum officinale

Jasmine takes its name from the Persian word *yasamin*. Its place of origin is not known, for sure, but it is most likely Persia.

In China, where it has been known since the third century AD, it is considered a foreign plant. For the Chinese the jasmine was a symbol of womanly sweetness.

It was certainly well-known to ancient Greeks and Romans. In the first century AD, Discorides mentions it in the *Materia Medica*, saying that Persians used it to perfume the air at banquets.

It is said that a few drops of jasmine oil massaged on the body with some almond oil helps overcome frigidity, and that dreaming of jasmine is supposed to portend good fortune, especially in love.

MAGICAL USES   The little intensely scented jasmine has to be the flower of sensual love, of pleasure, of the joys of the senses, of enduring physical attraction between two people. Having this flower around, smelling its scent, looking at the fragile little white flower which is so strong in its smallness and prettiness, cannot fail to do good. If you are a woman, it will put you in touch with your feminine sexual instincts, your

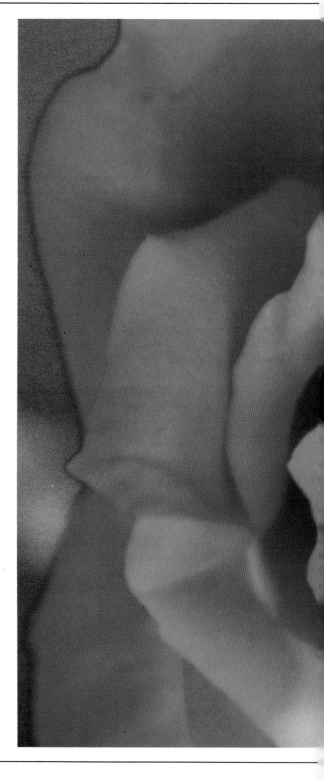

The simple name of the rose came originally from the Celtic word *rhodd*, meaning red. This word in turn became *rhodon* in Greek, which became *rosa* in Latin. There are many legends about this glorious flower including one of the most famous in which Achilles' shield displayed the flower.

desire to feel well in yourself and to look good and to enjoy this dance of the polarity of existence. Use jasmine then when you want to feel more attractive, when a love is new and sweet, or when it is old and mature but wants to find again the sweetness of its beginning.

Use jasmine in incantations for those women who have difficulty in opening themselves to the pleasures of the senses; those who are unaware of the beauty and sexiness of their own body. If the case is serious and there is a real problem of dislike for one's own physical form, make it stronger by using it in conjunction with herbs and/or perhaps stones.

It is a good flower to also use if you are doing magic for a man who wants to find a new love. This flower will open his heart to a new feminine presence in his life.

PRACTICAL INFORMATION Jasmine is a plant indigenous to the warm parts of the eastern hemisphere and now also cultivated in gardens in southern America. The flowers are used as a sedative according to old herbals. In India it is used as a remedy for snakebite.

ROSE
Rosa

The name rose comes from the Celtic *rhodd*

The flower which is as important as love itself — the rose will aid all incantations, all spells and all remedies for the heart. Carry the flower fresh, or the petals, or even rose essence or rose water, with you at all times when you have love in mind or in the heart.

which means red, from which derived the Greek *rhodon*, which is the origin of the Latin *rosa*. This name remains much the same in all European languages. There are no doubts about the ancient origin of this flower. In the Museum of the Rose, in the garden of Hay les Roses near Paris, rose fossils are preserved.

The first historical evidence of the rose is from the time of the Sumerians: their King, Sargon The First, who lived in 2684 B.C. talks about "trees of roses" which he brought back from an expedition beyond the river Tauro.

In Homer's *Iliad* the shield of Achilles was described as having roses designed on it. The story of the rose goes on from there, passing more recently through the War of the Roses in the England of Edward I.

Today the rose is as much in favor as ever, and there are innumerable varieties of it on the market, with florists forever trying to improve on the already perfect.

MAGICAL USES   Of course the rose cannot be missing from the altar of any magician who would use flowers as primary tools.

The rose is as well-known, as beautiful and as important as love is. And that is exactly her use in magic. Any love magic will use a rose, either alone or in conjunction with other remedies. It could be a red one for passionate affairs, a yellow one for tender ones (and sometimes for jealousies), a pink one for romance or a white one for a pure love.

Perhaps you are walking down the street and from a garden a pink rose peers at you in all her freshness and perfume. You pick it and take it home. You can be sure that a little romance is in store for you that day. Something very sweet and friendly is going to happen and it will keep on your lips the smile that began when you first saw the bud. Therefore, if you ever have the impulse to buy yourself a bunch of roses, be it red or white or pink, do not hesitate to follow that impulse; you will be helping nature on its way.

For incantations you can of course use the fresh flowers, as they are not difficult to find in the shop at any time of the year. But you can also use the essence of rose which is also easy to get, and it is quite helpful for "quick magic". If love is in the air for you, carry a little bottle of rose water. A sniff of it before meeting the man or woman of your life will ensure your heart to be open and receptive, and ready to melt. If, when you sniff it, you close your eyes and remember the magic, it will give your whole being such a radiance that the other person will not fail to notice it (even though perhaps not consciously) and to answer it likewise.

Below
There are over one hundred known and named species of wild rose — all of which have been taken into cultivated flower production everywhere in the world. The rose is so popular that gardeners are constantly looking for ways to make new species.

Right
Of all flowers the tulip is one of the favorites, equalled only by the rose and the carnation. Tulips appear in songs and stories and most of us are very happy to have their presence and their fragrance in our homes.

To prepare a full incantation with roses, prepare yourself in the usual way and call the powers. Depending on the element answering you, you will choose the appropriate magic. You might write a spell and place it under the

rose bud; you wait until it is totally open: at that moment the magic will be accomplished. You might burn rose essence, or bathe in rose petals. Or if you have more time and you want a really special magic, wait for all the right factors to be present (the moon, the winds, etc.), plant a seed, and wait until the first flower blossoms. This last one is good to do

when starting a new love affair. The rose plant will mirror and protect your new love. Nourishing it and feeding it, and watching it grow tall and full of flowers you will be caring for and looking at your own love life. It will carry you through in times of misunderstanding, when watching the plant still beautiful and rich, you will know that there is nothing to worry about. And it will warn you if there is something wrong, if the plant looks like it needs water or medicines or a different lighting, you will be aware of your relationship needs even before they manifest themselves in conflicts.

PRACTICAL INFORMATION   There are over one hundred species of roses which are found wild and they are also widely cultivated all over the world. Red roses are considered best for medicinal uses: as astringent, gastric, for headaches, for sore throats, as a heart and nerve tonic and as a blood purifier.

TULIP
Tulipa

The word *tulipa* seems to be a degeneration of the name by which the Turks called the headdress of the Slavonian, which is *tlban* or *turban*. In fact the origin of this flower is in the East, and there it started its career about a

The tulip is magical for mending breaks — of the heart. It is not normally found in the magic grimoires but its magic certainly lies in its scent and if there is some split with the loved one, it will aid the repair.

---

thousand years ago. It grew wild in Persia. A Persian legend says that the tulip grew from the spilled blood of a lover, and for a long time a tulip symbolized a love declaration.

After a slow start, when it was introduced in Europe around 1500, the interest for this new flower developed into a real "tulipomania". In fact at the end of that century at Lille a brewer gave his whole brewery for a bulb, and the brewery was from then on called the Brasserie Tulipe. Today tulips, specially the Dutch ones, are very well-known and still loved flowers.

MAGICAL USES The tulip is not a flower which you will ever find in any witch's grimoires — nor does it traditionally have any magical associations. But it has a magical essence, like all flowers, and it is a strong and beautiful one.

The tulip has the power to mend breaks — of the heart, that is. If you have argued with your beloved, or your friend, and you wish to put an end to the struggle, use the power of the tulip to help you. The tulip has a beauty of its own, uncomplicated and simple, with a quality of firmness and honesty to it. All this comes through when you are using it for magic, and it is the best glue that you can find.

The best way of using them in your magic is to prepare yourself as usual, and then to take an object of your own, and one belonging to the other person; bring them into the circle, together with the tulips. Lay the objects together, place one of the flowers over them, and pronounce these words:

All wrongs to cease

All fractures repaired

With the tulip my friend

Let this bonding be spared.

You will need to do no more, and the peace is made.

PRACTICAL INFORMATION Tulips are available all year round in shops. They are also quite easy to grow, even at home on the windowsill, and it is advisable to have one around at all times.

The Magic of Stones

Diamonds, topaz, rubies, agate, quartz; embedded in earth's bowels are the most cherished of her treasures. Precious and semiprecious stones lie in silent splendor with no other merit than their beauty, no other use than being precious.

From the times of the Aztecs and the Incas (possibly long before) precious stones have been extracted to be worn or just admired by fortunate people who would treasure them above all other possessions. From those times, with their rare and aloof quality, precious and semi-precious stones have been representing that part of human life which has an intrinsic worth — that which is worthy because it is beautiful and it lasts; that whose usefulness lies in spiritual necessities rather than in physical or emotional ones. Therefore stones have always lent themselves as excellent primary tools of magic.

They are like flowers in as far as their meaning is in their beauty — but unlike flowers, they last a very long time, if not forever. For this, where flowers can be easily compared to emotions, stones are similar to the gifts of the spirit — whose incomparable worth lies in their own intrinsic, lasting, preciousness.

Stones in magic can be used when you want to operate on the deeper parts of reality, on the spiritual plane. An issue can affect you on a simply physical plane. For example, the need for a better job could be a purely material consideration, and/or can affect you emotionally — if you are looking for an activity which improves your connection with people, or where you can expand more on a heart level. Yet the same issue can also affect you spiritually — where your need for a different job would be the expression of a much deeper need for a change in the direction of your life.

Maybe a cycle of experiences has come to an end for you and you are starting a new one...and the change of the job is an outward expression of this profound need.

Much in our lives affects us in this way: it does not always have to do with radical life changes, but also with changes in perspective on one particular issue, in deep healing processes, in a deepening of the understanding. Therefore stones are often used in magic. Their powers are deep and lasting. When for example, you use gold to open yourself to abundance in the universe and in your own life, the chances are that it will not be just an inheritance of fifty dollars from your Aunt Mary that will fall on you, but that you will change the pattern of your life to accommodate a larger possibility for wealth.

Stones are beautiful and valuable and should thus be retained in a beautiful and secure place. It is also not good for them to be picked up by just anyone, for this way they will lose their strength and their power.

Here we cannot examine all the precious and semi-precious stones, so a selection of them and a method of working with them are given. Recognizing the stones; those which will work best for you and in what area, again depends largely on you. You might agree or not agree with my interpretation of a stone, and the way I use it for magic. The point here again is, like for all primary tools, to find your own magical relationship with them.

KEEPING YOUR MAGIC STONES

You need a beautiful, special place to keep your stones in: perhaps a wooden box, lined with velvet or satin, or a large flat tray of wood or ceramic. If the stones are many and money is short even a simple basket will do, lined with a pretty cotton. Keep them covered. And, of course, put them safely away. You must avoid people picking them up and toying with them out of curiosity.

USING STONES FOR MAGIC

Really precious stones have a strong and permanent effect in magic, but semiprecious and even ordinary ones also possess magical powers waiting to be released.

For example, a ruby will speak to you of love and passion, and so will a red jasper. Naturally if you do have a ruby and can use it, so much the better, but the humbler red jasper can have the same effect. Considering that, in the end, the first and only real requirements of magic are intensity and concentration, you are a lot better off with the right atmosphere and a lesser stone than with the most precious diamond and a distracted attitude.

If you choose stones as a primary tool for your magic you need to have a wide collection of them. As I said before they need not be expensive, but you do need to have a wide range of different ones. You need to be totally sure that stones are what you want as a primary tool for your magic. Stones do not "speak" to everybody: it could be that your liking for them is superficial. In this case you would not obtain many results working with them — as with all primary tools the depth of the connection is what you need to be looking for.

Since stones connect with the deepest level of reality, perhaps it is not a good idea to choose them as your first primary tool or to experiment with them if you are still not too sure of your ground.

CHOOSING YOUR STONES

Give yourself plenty of time when you go out to choose your stones. Plan on getting them over a long period; you should not be choosing more than one or two in one day. You need to have quite a good selection of stones for magic. Consider these main categories: love; money; career, work; health; family matters; religion, meditation, spiritual life; relationship to oneself; relationship to others; travel; bureaucracy.

You can of course make up your own reference list, corresponding to what your needs are, but if you need something to get started on, the above gives you a good idea of the various walks of life you are going to want to choose your stones for.

For example, you go out to choose a stone for travel matters. You will look at and feel different ones with that subject in your mind. You will see that one of them responds exactly to what you require. It is possible that more than one stone will "speak" to you on that subject, specially when you are considering work or love or health issues which in themselves are very broad categorizations. In this case pay even closer attention. Probably for you one stone is related to the creative aspect of work, another to the financial aspect and so forth.

In the end your collection of stones should be able to answer all of your requirements.

GOLD AND SILVER

Although gold and silver are minerals and not stones, I include them under this heading as primary tools. They are, in fact, largely available in normal households and can be safely and easily used for magic (see chart at end of section).

STONES AS GIFTS

If a stone has been given to you as a gift it possesses an extra quality given to it by the care of the person who has given it to you.

It is possible, even desirable, to use in magic

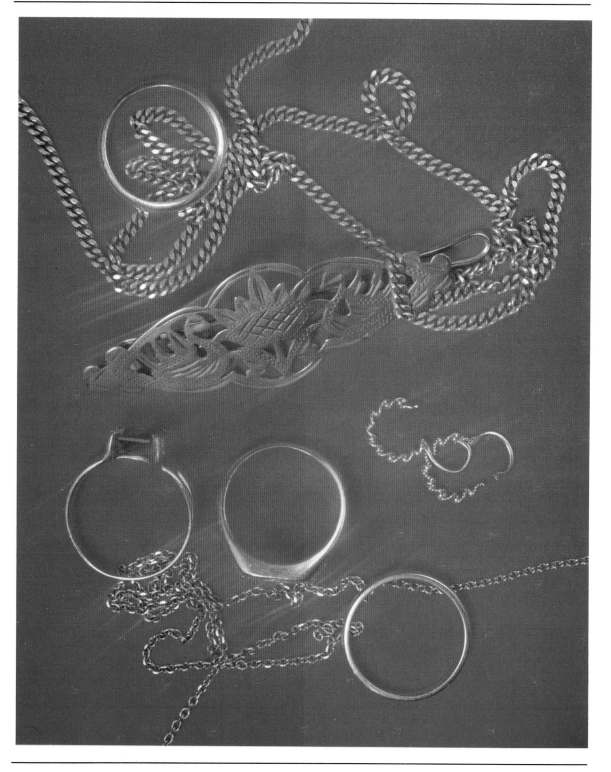

Left
Although not stones, gold and silver metals are needed in the magic related to stones. Their intrinsic value makes them of equal merit to precious stones.

Below
Purifying the stones should be performed in natural surroundings using natural resources — pure source water, linen cloth and the sun.

stones which are set to be worn; a sapphire in a ring is as good for magic as a loose stone.

However, you should be careful about using the stone given to you by someone who is trying to manipulate you through that gift, someone who does not give out of love or friendship, but out of calculation. If you really like it and want to use it anyway, cleanse it first with a purification ritual. A good one is the following:

TO PURIFY A STONE

Find a fresh-water source in nature and take your stone to it. Let the water wash over the stone for a few minutes. You can hold it in your hand (the left one) or, if it is too cold, lay it on the water bed, somewhere where the water is shallow and you can easily see it. During this time be silent and direct all your thoughts to the stone you are purifying. Imagine the fresh water meeting the stone and washing away all past experiences which might have accumulated on it. Wrap the stone in a clean white linen cloth and take it home, where you will keep it exposed to the rays of the sun for three days. This period is important because it "warms up" your stone and wakens her powers. If you don't have a garden or balcony, the windowsill will

do. After this your stone will be clear of any possible negative memory and will be ready for you to use.

WAYS OF USING STONES

As you have seen in the introduction of this section the first step is always the Calling the Powers ritual. Using your primary tool for the magic does not change the procedure, except' for the fact that you might want to have with you the tool you intend using. Keep it either inside the circle, if you have drawn one, or together with the symbols of the elements, or in your hand. In the latter case the hand should be the left one.

Depending on which element has "answered you", you will choose an appropriate procedure to follow. Here are some examples of how to use your stones in magic. These only want to be suggestions, as you alone can finally tell what the magic is showing you. These suggestions are based on the magic of the four elements as explained in part one.

If your chosen element is fire: the example shown in the introduction, in which you use the warm glow of a candle to bring to life the energy of your stone, is a good way of using your stone in the ambit of fire.

Wearing a stone on your body, either in the form of a piece of jewelry, or an amulet — perhaps kept in a small muslin pouch, and hidden in a pocket — is perhaps the best known and most ancient method of using stones for magic. Giving a ring as an engagement token is an act of magic, unconscious perhaps, but still magic. You charge the stone you are giving with your intent of making the

relationship last and remain happy. While that stone is worn it will act as a subtle, constant reminder of the vow taken to each other and it will build a subtle body of magic around the two people who have shared the gift. If the engagement is broken the ring should be removed. The intent is not there anymore, the magic useless.

An engagement ring does a lot, even though in most cases the people giving it are totally unaware of the magic they are operating. Think how much stronger such a thing can work when the magic is consciously intended!

You can wear any kind of stone in this way — except perhaps tektite and iron pyrite. After having consecrated the stone in the opening ritual (charging it with the energy of your intent) decide how long you want to wear it. For this magic it is good to choose the appropriate phase of the moon to begin. If, for example, your intent is to find a new love, choose the waxing moon, and remove the stone (perhaps a ruby or a red jasper or maybe a garnet) when the moon is full.

Another good way of using a stone — this time in the correspondence with water — is the following very simple one: your stone, a tiger's eye for this example, should be scrupulously clean for the purpose. After having called the

powers, place the stone in the cup in front of
you. Dip the finger tips of your left hand into
the cup and wet the point in the middle of your
forehead. Tiger's eye is the stone of independence. As you wet your forehead let one image
flood your mind of what independence at this
moment means to you. You might see yourself
working at your computer — or swimming laps
in the pool. Or you might receive the image of a
person laughing merrily.

Whatever the image tells you, consider it
carefully and follow it to your best ability.
While you are doing this, it is a good idea to
keep the tiger's eye with you, or to keep it on
your bedside, or under your pillow. It will give
you the strength to follow your intuition and
the clarity to understand what you need to
know.

The following method of magic is one which
some of you might experiment with at one time
or another. It deals with the element air.

Let us say you are a woman of childbearing
age, and at this moment feel you are ready to
give birth to a child. You desire it to be a girl.

Sit in your magic place. This time you know
beforehand that you will be using a spell in your
magic — spells belong to the realm of air. You
don't need to call the elements, but can just
look at the incense — or whatever else your

symbol for air is — and salute air. Write the
words of your wish on to an apposite clean,
white, unrolled piece of paper. Make them
simple and direct. You could write, for example:

To you girl my body is open,

To you girl my heart is open,

To you girl my mind is open,

Come.

Fold up the paper and place it in a special box
that is clean and used only for this purpose. Put
a blue laced agate and rose quartz together with
the paper. The agate is the stone of girls, the
quartz a healing stone for the body, which
makes it receptive.

Close the box and put it away somewhere
near you, for example in the bedroom or in the
living room if it is not used by too many people.
Naturally if you have a magic room you should
keep it there.

Consider beforehand the time span of the
spell. This can be a fairly long one. Start with
the waxing moon and wait for a whole cycle of
the moon, until it is again at the same phase.
Your wish will be fulfilled.

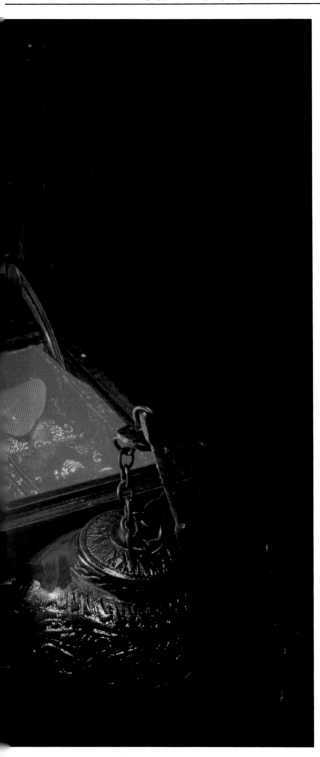

For those wishing to give birth to a girl-child, the special box, a blue laced agate stone and a rose quartz are the tools needed. The agate is the stone for girls, the quartz for healing of the body and the box will contain your own special energy.

This is a reminder: magic cannot work against the law of nature, it works with it. If you are not fertile, and cannot conceive, no magic will help you — you should see a specialist. If you are "helping the stars", that is, if you are just waiting for it to happen and want to help things along, and maybe want to have a say about the sex of the baby, you can be sure that this magic will make your dreams come true.

The various stones:

AMETHYST

This is one of the most beautiful varieties of quartz whose shades go from very dark violet to pale rose. Although the darkest shades are the most appreciated, the rose-lilac variety is also very beautiful.

This is the spiritual stone par excellence. It aids the ability to develop and evolve spiritually; therefore it is good to use it when invoking help for meditation and for rising above daily problems. To sleep with an amethyst under the pillow is said to relieve insomnia, promote dreams and inspired thinking.

Amethyst is therefore the stone to use when you are using dreams in your magic. It is not the stone to use when you want to promote a

If you have chosen to use the element of fire with your stone for magic, then the warm glow of a candle will bring life and energy to the stone.

strong passion. In fact, if your intent is to find someone to fall madly in love with, you should stay well clear of amethysts!

AQUAMARINE

The pretty blue aquamarine has the same composition of the far more precious emerald, and it is only less valuable because it is found more abundantly in nature. It is said that a true aquamarine is recognizable by putting it in the sea water, because it disappears — its color and transparency matching perfectly that of the sea. Hence its name. The darker the color the more precious is the stone: the dark blue ones are the most sought after.

Aquamarine has a clear, very soothing, cool energy. It promotes clarity of mind and it is specially helpful when this clarity has been impaired by a strong emotion, like anger or fear. In this case just holding the aquamarine in your hands and looking at it, will help you regain your composure. Its cool collected quality can also be a very good influence on you if you are going for an examination, or a job interview.

Aquamarine can also be used in magic for healing the body. It is, in fact, an excellent cleanser and purifier, to be used in incantations when health is impaired through stress and tensions, or through excesses in food, alcohol, smoke or drugs. It is also very effective in magic dealing with impurities of the skin — the aquamarine will give your skin its pure transparency.

AGATE

This stone comes in many different varieties of color, patterns and opacity. It takes its name from that of the river where it was originally found: Achatès.

It is generally an energy booster, but its various forms have different energies and different ways of being used in magic. Ursula Markham in her book *Fortune Telling by Crystals and Semiprecious Stones* considers the stones and the way they can tell her about other people and where they are at. In many cases I share her feeling about a stone, and how I use it in magic is often similar to the way she uses it in divination. Anyway her book is a work which I highly recommend to anyone who chooses stones for their primary tools.

AGATE GEODE

This stone has the power to open your psychic

powers, it is therefore a very important one in magic. It is not likely that you will be attracted to it if you are not already predisposed towards psychic work anyway — but if you are, and you acquire an agate geode, by keeping it on your bedside you will be able to nourish those qualities while you sleep. As you open more and more to the world of the psyche, you will feel your connection with your stone grow stronger and stronger.

Use it in incantations where those powers are needed — maybe to reveal to you the true situation of a loved one away from you, or to discover the potential of a new situation.

BOTSWANA AGATE

A very nice stone to have! This beautiful stone of delicate colors and patterns always brings with it happy news.

Use it in incantations when you are depressed and feeling low. It will be like giving yourself a present — of a magical nature! In fact by using this stone and wishing for something nice and unexpected to happen, you are always in for a happy surprise.

This stone does not comport deep changes or great revolutions. Your gift will be of a very transitory nature, but nevertheless it will be

The blue laced agate carries the energy of a young girl — delicate and soft — and may work well for a man who seeks the love of a young woman.

like a smile brightening up a dreary day. Perhaps a long-lost friend will pay you a visit or you might be given a bunch of flowers by an unknown admirer... or you will discover that you have lost three pounds in weight! With such magic it is important that you be careful not to overdo it, and if you are operating the magic for someone else remember that you will not be able to claim any merit, as the gift is always of a totally unobtrusive and natural nature.

MOSS AGATE

This soft collard stone with the strange arabesques brings with it peace of mind and the end of a period of anxiety. It is definitely the stone to use when things are getting to be too much to bear. It's good to use it together with another banishing element, for example, the waning moon and the north wind. Just see all your problems being blown away by the wind, and place the stone on your window sill while the moon is waning... with the moon your problems will also decrease, and when the moon is empty they will be gone. Then take your moss agate, purify it using the method described above and put it away safely until you need it again.

AGATE WITH FOSSILS

A very interesting one. While gold is directly connected with the feeling of abundance in the universe and opens you to the possibility of a greater abundance in your life, this stone deals more particularly with inheritances, precious gifts, possessions.

Like the fossils embedded in the stone, giving it its beauty and preciousness, so life's material riches are supposed to be ornamental to your life, not curtailing your freedom, but simply enabling you to enjoy it more. When money or riches or any kind of inheritance or possession is a burden to you, use this stone in your incantation and you will be able to again find your balance and your truth with them.

BLUE LACED AGATE

This is the loveliest stone, of a delicate, pretty blue color, with soft veining running along it. It is the stone of a girl child — says Ursula Markham — and indeed the feeling of this stone is of the softest, most delicate energy.

It is a good stone to use in many different ways. A good example is that of a man who wants to fall in love — use this stone in the incantation to help him find a girl, provided

that he goes for the soft, feminine type of girl. Should he be looking for a strong independent character, I should rather use a different stone, like the tiger's eye.

This stone is also successfully used in magic related to other people. If someone you know and care for is really overbearing and aggressive, you might do a lot of good to everybody by doing a little magic with this stone over that person. To do magic about other people, when they do not ask you for it, is *always* dodgy. It is something to be very careful about, as you never really know how pure your intentions might be, and you could be trying to manipulate someone into doing something or being something they do not want to do or be. In this context the blue lace agate is one of the safest stones to use on someone else. All you would be doing is bringing a little mellowness to a situation.

If you want to know the sex of an unborn baby: ask the mother to close her eyes and to pick one of the two — a blue lace agate or a quartz agate. A choice of the first denotes the presence of a baby girl, the second of a boy.

AMETHYSTINE AGATE

This stone brings with it the "winds of change". It is a change that, starting with the gift of new inner perspective usually expresses itself in a move: a move of home, a long trip abroad, a stay in a different country.

Use this in magic in relationship to yourself or/and others, when you feel you are getting stale and life is becoming boring for you. This is a sure symptom, and a very common one, that life's forces are somehow sleeping in and around you and that you need to shift yourself, see things from a different perspective and bring fresh energies into your life.

TURQUOISE

This blue-green stone has been used as a good luck charm since the most ancient times. But it must always be given in gift by someone; it cannot be purchased or it will loose its magical powers.

It was sacred to the American Indians and used in jewels in ancient Egypt and in Byzantium. The Aztecs considered this stone so important that they valued a man's reputation from the number of turquoises that he possessed.

The influence of this stone is indeed a powerful and happy one. It is above all protective. It has the gift of sustaining the peace and contentment of the spirit against all hurt and peril. A gift of this stone to a new baby, or a new home, is always right, as you would be giving a promise of peace and serenity, contentment and lasting pleasure.

Use it in magic when facing troubled times and when your inner peace is at stake. If you recognize the danger and make an incantation using this stone before things have gone too far, you will surely shelter your balance and contentment. Do not, however, make the mistake of thinking that you can get yourself out of mischief by using this stone. If you are already feeling bad, are depressed, sad, etc. use a bloodstone to relieve the symptoms of depression. Find out the causes of your ill-being and then use the appropriate stone to set things right again. Turquoise is a protective stone, which will maintain a state of happiness and fend off possible unhappy situations.

JASPER

Jasper was one of the stones used by the ancient Egyptians, who used to put it on the bodies of their dead. They believed that it had the power to accompany the dead on their journeys into the other world.

A one colored jasper is rare, as it usually presents a mixture of colors. Of the colored ones — red jasper is the most valued. But the green with red is also well considered. The various differently colored jaspers have different uses in magic.

RED JASPER

The stone of strong healthy feelings, of love and passion and strong emotions. Needless to say this is the stone (as well as the ruby) to use in love magic. If a heart is cold and needs warmth, use this stone. It is also a good stone to be used if the body is cold, either due to an illness or to inhibited sexual responses. Give a red jasper to your lover to ensure that passion stays alive between you.

If you are an over-passionate person, who rather needs clarity than passion, stay clear of the red jasper or you might find yourself in more heated situations than you had bargained for.

BLOODSTONE

This stone is a very deep dark red which nearly looks black.

It helps to overcome those states of depression and melancholia due to a general lowering

Left
The two most precious varieties of "corundum" are ruby and sapphire and they are the hardest stones in the world apart from the diamond. Although the most pure rubies cannot be acquired by any but the richest, the less pure examples are easily available and most useful for magic.

Below
Quartz concentrates the rays of the sun and can therefore be used for crystal magic and pendulum magic. The stone is also known as "sacred fire".

of the body's vital energy. It is a stone to be used carefully as it has a strong effect, and it is a bit like a medicine. Use it only as long as you need it, and then put it safely away. It is like an injection of strength... while under the magical influence of this stone you will probably find yourself looking for certain foods — which your body must be feeling a need for — or craving for certain occupations. You must absolutely follow those impulses, as this is the way the powers of the stone are healing you.

It is best if you can initiate your magic at sunrise. Choose to start on the first day of a weekend so that you have two fairly free days to follow the energy of the stone.

RUBY

The corundum comes only after the diamond for hardness. Its two most precious varieties are the ruby and the sapphire. Rubies have been extracted as early as the fourth century in Burma and in Sri Lanka and have always been one of the most valued stones. Really pure rubies are very hard to find and very precious; their color goes from a delicate rose-violet to a deep dark red. The most valued variety presents a bright, strong color: pigeon blood.

While only the richest can permit themselves a totally pure, big ruby, lesser varieties are easily available and can be equally used in magic. Of course any magician would be absolutely thrilled at the possibility of working with a pure, true, precious gem, such as a ruby, a diamond, a sapphire. I guess you can see it as the difference between going somewhere in a

Place a piece of quartz next to your head on your pillow, during an afternoon sleep or at night, if you have a headache. Quartz will naturally clear your head and relieve the tension that brought the headache in the first place.

Rolls Royce, and going there in a Deux Chevaux. The aim is equally achieved. There is just an extra special pleasure in handling a pure gem and feeling its unequaled power, its history, its radiant beauty.

Ruby is the stone of love and passion between man and woman and of sexual love. A ruby as an engagement ring means a lot! The red jasper which we have seen before also has the property of promoting love, but the love of the ruby is somewhat more intense and less earthy. Jasper's love is the one which gives birth to children and home, ruby's love to poems and great deeds. Using both stones in an incantation would indeed be giving a very strong intention to it!

In the choice between red jasper and ruby, if you have them both, you should rather let your intuition lead you than trying to work out what kind of love you are doing magic for.

QUARTZ CRYSTAL

Here is a very useful stone in magic. Crystal quartz is the material used for crystal balls, pendulums and other objects of magic.

A property of this stone is to concentrate the rays of the sun, and for that reason it was called "sacred fire". Indeed, the principal gift of this stone is that of aiding concentration. It helps you concentrate your strength and powers on your chosen subject — as concentration is the first requirement of magic, you can see why this mineral would be chosen for magical objects.

The quartz crystal can also work similarly on the body, by helping you to focus all healing energies on the part you wish to cure. For quick relief from a headache, try lying down placing a quartz crystal on the pillow near your head. As this stone helps you concentrate your efforts and succeed, it is also a good one to use in weight loss incantations.

Besides for healing, use it in those matters where you need to concentrate your strength and resources. Preparing for examinations or meeting deadlines. Quartz crystal helps you to reach success in those endeavors where your work alone is what matters. When forced to make a difficult choice use this stone together with the aquamarine to give you the clarity to see what is right and the strength to carry it through.

SAPHIRE

This is another of the varieties of the corundum, together with the ruby. It is also highly esteemed — specially when its color is an

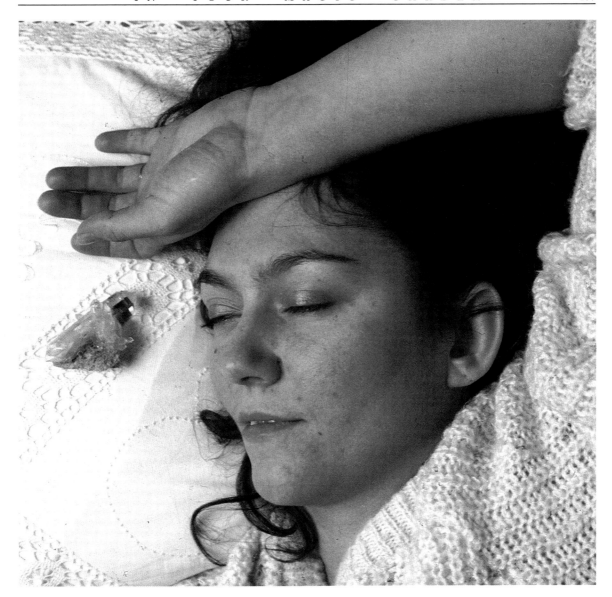

intense blue-azure and remains the same which-ever side you are looking at.

This is a very important stone if you are on a spiritual path. It favors enlightenment, pro-motes spiritual devotion, protects the mind from madness and gives it courage. If you have the good fortune to possess a sapphire, use it in incantations when you want to find or help someone find a "meaning" in what they are doing.

Today's social conditioning can produce am-bition without understanding. When the goal is reached a great confusion arises — what have you worked and spent your energies for; why did you get where you are now in the first place? Often people find themselves at this

Infinite possibilities of increasing creativity in any area, rutilated quartz can also work with other stones, for example with quartz crystals to concentrate your creative efforts.

point, and what results from it is often stress, tension, anxiety. In this case sapphire must be the magical stone of this century. Under the influence of this stone appropriately used in incantations, you can help yourself or someone else, to again find the thread of your life.

This is a long project in most cases which will need a careful combination of magical elements and several sessions. And, of course, the sapphire is not an easy stone to come by. A good idea when you have several friends who are interested in using stones for good magic is to get together and buy a "communal" sapphire — which shall be kept somewhere and used only for magic. It does not have to be a big one, even a very small stone will do, and you can find a good, fairly pure, small gem for varying prices.

RUTILATED QUARTZ

This is a beautiful quartz with honey colors and gold threads running through it. It is the stone of creativity, therefore a must in anybody's stones collection. Rutilated quartz brings the gift of finding one's own creative potential, be it in art or writing or poetry or cooking or gardening. The possibilities are infinite.

Use rutilated quartz when you want to

discover what your creative potential is. Or if you are already engaged in a creative activity and you are in the last throes of a project, you can use it together with a quartz crystal to be able to concentrate all your energies on your talents. Or you could use it together with a happy stone such as turquoise, to bring happiness and serenity into your work. The rutilated quartz lends itself to numerous beautiful combinations.

FLUORITE OCTAHEDRON

This interestingly shaped stone is the one of work and business enterprises. It is a stone which will help you channel your energies in a productive way, such as engaging yourself in the working world. You can safely use the octahedron whenever you are performing any kind of working magic. Used alone it will ensure that your focus remains on work, if this is what you need or desire. Together with other stones it can give a more specific aim to your working magic.

For example, the octahedron used in conjunction with the rose quartz will help you find, or succeed in, a healing career — be it that of a surgeon or nurse, or that of a spiritual healer. To be more specific, use an amethyst if you

wish your career to be that of a spiritual healer, or a jasper — a brown jasper — if you are more interested in curing the body. Either way it will be an occupation which you shall make into something viable and which will actively occupy you.

TIGER'S EYE

This beautiful stone resembling the eye of a tiger gives confidence to who wears it. It brings the ability to understand oneself and the strength to express one's understanding.

Use it in incantations to help shyness or when setting out on one's own, and after a separation — when the mourning period is over and life is ready to start again. It is a good stone to give as a gift to adolescents ready to become free individuals.

IRON PYRITE

This is called "fool's gold" because of its apparent resemblance to the noble mineral. It is in fact a lot harder than gold, slightly darker in color and far less noble!

Iron pyrite is a stone of deception and misunderstanding. You must be very careful, therefore, when you use it in magic; it can be useful but only in certain cases and with the right precautions. Use it when you need to conceal your actions or your intentions. Cases where self-concealment is good are rare, and you must be very sure when you choose to do such a magic that you are not causing any harm to yourself and others. For this reason when using the iron pyrite put the stone of clear thinking and awareness — the aquamarine — next to it. This you need to do *every time* you use iron pyrite in an incantation.

An example of a case in which you might want to use iron pyrite is an incantation to assure the good outcome of a new business venture, whose success depends largely on reaching the market prior to any leaks of information. In this case use the iron pyrite, the aquamarine and the octahedron — the stone of success in work and business ventures. Another example would be the launch of a new formula, book, perfume or other project, which needs secrecy to be completed without the idea being stolen. Here you would use the iron pyrite, the aquamarine and the rutilated quartz — the stone of creative work. Still another case, very likely, is that in which you might want to take a well deserved holiday and want to make absolutely sure that no one knows where you are; to avoid the risk of being

pestered with last minute emergencies, use iron pyrite, aquamarine and the labradorite — the stone of happy travel and/or holidays.

ROSE QUARTZ

This pretty rose crystal is the stone of healing and healers. The healing might be physical or emotional or spiritual. This stone should always accompany other stones or tools that you are using for a healing magic.

For example, you should use the rose quartz in conjunction with the appropriate herb to re-establish health in the convalescing period of a long illness. Or together with the yellow jasper (jealousy stone) to heal a sore heart. It is of course a nice present for a nurse or a doctor... but anybody can use the pretty rose quartz as a soft, healing presence around them.

STONES CHART

This chart lists precious and semiprecious stones together with their properties and uses in magic. I have talked about a few of them in detail before, giving examples of their uses. Some I have not talked about and they are given below for you to find out more about them, when you are interested!

STONE	NAME	PROPERTIES	MAGICAL USE
	TIGER'S EYE	Gives strength of character, banishes fears related to self.	Independence, divorce and separating magic. Starting off in business.
	AMETHYST	Spiritual stone, develops and evolves spirituality.	To help meditation, use in dream magic.
	ROSE QUARTZ	Healing.	Use in all healing magic, also together with other tools.
	BLUE LACED AGATE	Promotes softness and femininity.	To make soft, to become more feminine (if you should want to), to discover the sex of an unborn baby.
	BOTSWANA AGATE	Brings gifts and small pleasures.	When low in spirits, for a quick magical "pick me up".
	RED JASPER	Promotes earthy love and family feelings.	To attract a love affair, to warm up a body or a soul, to keep the passion hot.
	RUBY	High voltage love and passion.	To bring about a very deep and pure love affair.
	OCTAHEDRON	Channels energy into work.	Use by itself to focus on work, together with other stones to achieve different working goals.

STONE	NAME	PROPERTIES	MAGICAL USE
	GARNET	Heightens sexual awareness.	Opening oneself to life's pleasures and to sex.
	JADE	Brings beauty.	In beauty magic, to discover one's own beauty.
	OPAL	Stone of the spirits.	To get in touch with the spirit world.
	TURQUOISE	Protective, maintains health and happiness.	To protect yourself when facing hard times, a good luck charm, a beautiful gift.
	SAPPHIRE	Gives peace of mind, favors enlightenment.	For confusion, to help find lost truths.
	EMERALD	Future seeing.	Divination.
	TOPAZ	Courage and warmth.	Dispelling fears with the light and warmth of love.
	LAPIS LAZULI	Children.	Improving child-adult relations, fertility.

STONE	NAME	PROPERTIES	MAGICAL USE
	PETRIFIED WOOD	Brings clarity in legal matters and bureaucratic work.	Lawsuits, success as a lawyer, secretary stone.
	IRON PYRITE	Deception and misunderstanding.	When needing to conceal, when wanting to "disappear" for a time, for business ventures and new projects. Use carefully.
	TEKTITE	Has banishing properties, sucks up bad energies.	Use in banishing magic, for hatred, jealousy, envy, anger, etc.
	AQUAMARINE	Clears the mind, cooling, purifying.	To regain composure, to think clearly, purifies the skin, to be cool in situations when it is important to be that way: examinations, interviews, etc.
	MOSS AGATE	Brings peace of mind, ends anxiety.	When things are getting too much, in incantations to relieve anxiety.
	RUTILATED QUARTZ	Promotes creativity.	To find out your creative potential, to help creativity.
	AGATE WITH FOSSILS	Integrates riches and inheritances, sudden increases of wealth.	To help finding a balance with one's own riches (a rich man's stone).
	BLOODSTONE	Injection of strength, relieves depression.	To relieve depression.

STONE	NAME	PROPERTIES	MAGICAL USE
	AGATE GEODE	Opens psychic powers.	When you need psychic powers.
	QUARTZ CRYSTAL	Concentrating.	Many, helps you concentrate your efforts to reach success in all fields, including healing magic.
	DIAMOND	Indomitable strength, everlasting ties.	To make incantations totally solid and lasting. Use with prudence.
	MOONSTONE	The stone of the night.	To enjoy night's gifts, shadows, dreams, silence.
	BROWN JASPER	The stone of the body.	To direct the energy towards the body.
	AMETHYSTINE AGATE	Moving, Changing.	To use against staleness and boredom.
	GOLD	Attracts abundance and richness.	To open yourself to abundance.
	SILVER	Makes you appreciate the purity and simplicity of poverty.	To appreciate poverty and its gifts.

Enchanted World

Even now
The night is full of silver straws of rain
and I will send my soul to see your body.

In this section you will see all that you have read about so far combined in a useful way. You must remember when using these incantations, that what is going to make your magic work is above all your intensity and your concentration. Without that, no matter how well you prepare your potions or how long you lie in the bath and repeat the right words, nothing is going to happen.

Although it is possible and enjoyable to perform magic with a partner, in this book are included only those incantations and rituals which are performed alone. There are two reasons for this: the first is that they are much

On a cold winter night, when searching through magic for a warm lover, it can be a pleasure simply to prepare, by the fire, all the items needed. The cleansing of your body, wearing new and clean clothes and laying out the special tools — all this is part of the magic.

simpler to practice in the early stage of learning. One person alone can make only so many mistakes. But bring another person, or two people and you will be in trouble. Secondly, to perform magic together with someone is a very delicate matter; you will have to take into consideration the energy of the other person. His or her degree of concentration and intensity must somehow match with yours, so that you can join together in a magical dance.

PREPARING YOUR INCANTATIONS

As you know from part one, there are many factors to be considered. Timing is one: whether you want to wait for the moon to wax or wane to begin your magic, whether a south or west wind might be helpful, if your magic should take place at sunrise perhaps or at sunset. Next, you need to know which tool you wish to use, and you have to find out what element is the best background for your purpose.

While the timing and the tools are to be determined prior to starting the magic, the appropriate element usually reveals itself in the course of the opening ritual Calling the Powers. In the course of this ritual you can also set the

details of the incantation, through knowledge and intuition. (It is worth remembering that certain herbs, or stones or flowers, call for a particular element — as I have specified before — in which case you will invoke the specific element, without waiting for one to speak to you).

As far as your own preparation is concerned it is important to be clean and properly clothed, and both your inner space and your outer one must be ready before you set off. It is not always necessary to perform the whole preparation routine for magic. As you will see from this section there are many opportunities for performing a quick magic pick up — or where a talisman or potion can be taken out and used at any moment of the day or night. Nevertheless there are bonuses which arise from a thorough and careful preparation at some other time. Magic needs dedication. You should devote one full session to it at least once a week, in which you follow the whole routine by cleansing, clothing, concentrating, calling the powers and so forth. That is the grounding and basis for all your magical practices.

Out of the following examples choose the ones which appeal to you most, and use them as stepping stones towards creating your own. Read on, and remember to have fun!

Wonderful Love

What would magic be for if it could not mend a broken heart, or make your lover love you as he or she should? For sure that is one of the first issues that everybody wants to explore once they have the ways and means. But remember, good magic is not to manipulate anyone or anything. And love is such a vast subject! The following examples are only a few simple steps of the magic dance in the tunes of love. They are all incantations and rituals to be performed by yourself. It is possible, and even advisable to perform love magic together with your partner or friend. But as it involves a further set of instructions and requirements, working with partners evades the scope of this book.

In any event to begin with, it is good to work alone. If you should make any mistakes, it will be only you to suffer the consequences!

TO AID A NEW LOVE

To begin a new love story is always exciting on the one side and a bit scary on the other. Let us say you have just met someone and all the signs are there. When your eyes meet something happens. Your body responds to the other person's body. You like these feelings, you

know something is going to happen in your life.
A new flower has just broken through and is
about to show its colors and give its fragrance
to the world. At this delicate stage you might
feel like you don't know what to say, what to
do. You might feel shy and embarrassed,
specially if you are a shy person anyway — or
one who is not so familiar with relating to the
opposite sex. You might even close yourself off
and risk putting an end to the whole affair
before it even starts.

Performing this magic ritual at such a time
can help in many ways. It will put you back in
touch with your very core; the place where your
confidence grows, and it will suffuse the whole
situation with helpful vibrations.

It is best to have a waxing moon for this
ritual, but it might be impractical to wait for
one, as this delicate phase of the beginning of a
new love might only last for as little as a few
days. Just see what the situation is. The ritual
involves about half an hour in the evening
before going to sleep and the same amount of
time in the morning. If you cannot manage to
get out of bed early, this ritual is not for you, as
the morning part of it *must* happen at sunrise.

In the evening, before going to sleep, cleanse
yourself and collect your thoughts and emotions. Dress for magic (possibly, this time,

wearing a simple white shift) and sit in your
magic space, facing the protector. Earlier that
day you will have provided one simple red rose,
which will now be in a vase in your magic
space, next to the protector, or in any event, at
your left. Let your eyes stay focused on the
protector, while your breath becomes slow and
steady. When you are calm and your mind is
free, call the elements as explained in part one.
When you come to the point of recalling the
purpose of your magic, and holding it in your
mind, it will be enough to visualize the face of
the person in question.

Let us say in this case the element fire will
answer you. Your new love affair will therefore
be a hot, passionate one. Prepare two red
candles for use in the morning. Check the time
the sun rises and using the visualization described in the Sun Magic morning ritual, let
yourself wake up naturally a few minutes before
sunrise.

As you rise, put something warm on — you
can wrap yourself up in a blanket — go outside
in the garden, if you have one or on the
balcony, or sit in front of an open window.
With a windsock and compass check what kind
of wind is blowing. If it is a west wind; gentle
and romantic, you are in luck — for this is
certainly a very good omen to the start of a

romance. An east wind is not a bad sign either, meaning that the new start will also expand in other areas of your life. A south wind is a bit hot and fiery for your purpose, unless you are the kind of person who can start off in fourth gear. But if the wind happens to be blowing from the north — it is better you postpone the whole thing to another day — as that is not at all a good sign for your purpose. The north wind is a wind of ending, of banishing, of empty restful periods.

Sit facing east, possibly in view of the rising sun. As you see the darkness being dispelled by the upsurging light, imagine your fears being within the last shadows of the night, and your heart in the coming sun. Place the rose in front of you. As you inhale the perfume say these words:

With you rose, my truest wishes are confided.

Then take the rose inside to your magic place, light the two candles and place them one on each side of the rose. They are to burn until the rose has fully flowered and is dead. If one set of candles is burned out, and the rose is still flowering, replace the candles with two fresh ones. Be very careful that the flames do not become extinguished while the rose is fresh, or the incantation will be broken. When the rose is completely dead, take it out of the water and place a few of the dried petals in your spell box, to stay there as safeguard to your love, until you have a need for them. Extinguish the candles then, and only then, by pinching (not by blowing).

There will now be nothing to fear either from yourself, or from outside circumstances to interfere with your new love. Magically protected, it will grow and bring joy to your life. There is, however, one thing to know about this incantation. I hope this will not happen to you, but if by chance, the flower should not open, and it should die before coming to full flowering, this would be an unmistakable sign that your new love affair will never get off the ground — and nothing you can do will prevent that!

TO CONJURE UP A LOVER

This incantation will come in very handy if you

A bonfire, a lock of your hair and a flask of good wine will aid the incantation of purification.

do not have a lover, but want one to hurry into your life. As this incantation is quite forceful, you must expect a stormy scene to present itself to you! Be careful though, not to be tempted to use this incantation on an old lover who perhaps for the time being is happier doing other things than being with you. Manipulating people and events, whether you do it by magic or not, is always something you are going to be sorry for, sooner or later. You might argue that you are already sorry now, and that the magic might relieve your depression. In this case you can do an incantation to relieve your sadness or grief, and wait to see what existence has in store for you. If you do magic to control someone, you might be relieved at the moment, but will be all the sorrier later on. *Never* misuse magic!

For this incantation you will use the red jasper: the stone of love and passion. It does not matter what time of the day or night you choose for this magic, but it will be good to wait for a hot south wind to blow. Prior to performing the magic, write this ancient spell on a piece of the appropriate paper which you keep for this purpose, with your special pen (see "Ordinary Tools"):

In three days

and three nights,
at this hour come.
Love come to my bidding.
Come in the red
amber of flame.
Come in the full
flooded moon of night.
Come to me in the
silent time of waiting.
Come on the violent
wings of tides.
In three days and
three nights,
at this hour,
to my bidding, come.

Keep the paper and the red jasper with you, cleanse and dress yourself and call the element fire. Hold the stone so that the light of the flames in the burner are flickering on it and warming up its spirit. Read the spell aloud, as you focus your total attention on the words you

are saying. Having done that, place the spell together with the stone in the spell box, and leave it there undisturbed for a whole moon cycle. By the time the moon is back to the same position, a love will have entered your life.

PURIFICATION SPELL

This is another fire magic, in this case, a bonfire magic. For this ritual you should best use an outside bonfire. (An indoor fireplace will be fine though, and failing even that, your burner will do).

Go to a mountain or a field, when the light of day is fading — in a time of waning moon. Bring with you a blanket and a flask of good wine, plus what you need to build a small bonfire. Also take with you a lock of your hair, already cut and tied with a ribbon, if the purification is for you, or a lock of the hair of the person you are doing the magic for.

When the fire is burning, sit in front of it, wrapping the blanket around you if it is cold. Sip a bit of your wine and feel the liquid going down inside your body. Feel how it spreads warmth and well-being. Relax looking at the fire for a while, only moving to kindle the

flames when needed. Then get up and, moving in circles around the fire, shake yourself until you feel your whole body alive and awake. Then sit down again and relax, looking at the flames, letting your mind be empty. Repeat the whole procedure a few times. At the end, when you sit down for the last time, you will be very awake, and at the same time very relaxed.

Now visualize the four elements and thank them as you do in the Calling the Powers ceremony. The element you are working with this time is fire. Take the lock of hair and visualize the face and body of the person they belong to — feel the presence of that person as if he or she was standing there next to you. Hold out the left hand containing the lock of hair over the fire (without burning yourself), and say these words of an ancient spell:

I touch the inner soul
of this man with my finger
I send the heat of the Mana
into his soul
I burn out all the coldness
I burn out all the suspicion
I burn out all the jealousy

I burn
    all the poison up
  all the dead things up
I burn through the
   shackles on love

he is changed,
    he is changed.

Finally throw the hair in the fire and see it burn. If you did this for yourself, feel your heart free and happy. Close your eyes and see yourself doing something out of this space of freedom and love: you might see yourself playing on an instrument, or traveling far away lands, or hugging someone. Whatever the image is, remember it, as later you will have to put your whole energy into making it come true.

If you were performing the magic for someone else, as you close your eyes let an image come of what this person most needs from you. It could be an image of you having fun together, perhaps going to the movies, or you could see yourself bringing warmth into the person's life — perhaps you are cooking a meal for that person. Or it could be that what is needed right now is to give freedom. As before,

follow the suggestions you have received in this way, as they come from the magic within you.

TO CURE A HURT
CAUSED BY LOVE

This is very simple: Take a few leaves of balm, it must be fresh; take your cup and go to a waterfall. It can be anytime of the day or night. As you reach your spot, sit there for a while, watching the water bubbling, and letting your heart hurt, without doing anything. Take some of the water into your cup, and put the leaves of balm in it. Balm has the property of soothing hurts and fears. As you drink the water, pronounce these words:

This water to heal,
this herb to soothe,
I am happpy again!

As you go back home, take with you a flask of the water from the waterfall. Place some fresh balm in a vase with that water and put it next to your bed. Leave it there for three nights. The third morning you will be well.

Take your chalice or, cup to a waterfall and sit watching the bubbling water for a while in silence — then follow the spell and a heart hurt by love will be cured.

FAMILY HAPPINESS

A happy family can be the source of the greatest pleasure in life. A simple, warm, tender life; enriched by the smiles of the children, by the pleasure of sharing one's trouble and victories, by the security of the knowledge of having a close partner always ready to take you to a place of rest and peace.

A family can make possible the enjoyment of those actions which are the most common and yet the most important in human life. Drinking tea, preparing a meal, or hanging a picture on the wall. In the cozy and safe atmosphere of a happy family those actions take a totally different quality, being relaxed and happy and enjoying them one can find the essence of contentment.

The following magic ritual will preserve the happiness of your family, and, more to the point, will help you appreciate its gifts, and will show you ways of restoring the harmony should it be impaired. This magic uses the power of earth, and should preferably be performed during the day, in the time of the waxing moon. The helpful winds would be westerly ones.

As you know from the section on stones magic, part two, the gift of a turquoise is one which can guarantee the safeguard of contentment and happiness. There should always be a turquoise in a family. It could be the gift of the man to the woman, or vice-versa, or it could have been given as birth present to any of the children, or simply as a house warming gift. The turquoise is essential in the magic ritual.

Also prepare an infusion mixing a few rosemary sprigs and hawthorn's flowers. You will have prepared this infusion beforehand taking care that it should be done in your house at night, with no electric light shining on the liquid, but only candles if the need arises. The reason for this is that the violent vibrations of the electric light might spoil the very subtle magical combination of rosemary and hawthorn, so compromising the power of the incantation.

The formulation of the magic itself does not take a long time. It can be therefore easily fitted between the activities of a weekend, for example, or even during a lunch break if you chance to go back home in that period. Remember though, that if you have been working or shopping, or otherwise have been engaged outside your home, you need to proceed carefully through the cleansing steps, and perhaps take a little longer over them — you need to remove the outside influences and vibrations from your own energy, which will be covering it and obscuring it just like the dust which you pick up in the streets.

Once you are ready, sit in front of the symbols of the elements and call the power earth, as it is earth which will work with you and for you in this magic. Raise the cup in which you will have poured some of your infusion of rosemary and hawthorn with both hands in front of you and call out these words:

From earth
My true home
These herbs I welcome!
With their powers
   they will show,
In peace and love
   the way to go.

Close your eyes and drink a few sips out of the cup. Then sit still and let the hawthorn and rosemary, the herbs of happiness and contentment, show you the ways of reaching love and contentment within your family.

As you know, the way herb magic works is to

A simple, warm tender family can be the greatest source of pleasure in life with the enriching presence of children and the opportunity to share one's troubles. There are many magic rituals for preserving family happiness.

feel your way around the cause of a long standing dispute with your partner. Pay close attention to these insights, as they are not ordinary intuitive glimpses, but the magic of earth, through the medium of herbs, speaking to you.

When you are ready pick up the turquoise, which was in front of you ready for use, place it in the rice bowl (or whatever else you use to represent the earth), and holding the bowl at the height of your heart "see" the turquoise become your "star guide" invested with the property of reminding you always of the contentment and happiness which resides somewhere in your heart, and which the magic of the rosemary and hawthorn have helped to bring to light momentarily.

The turquoise now will help guide your energy towards fulfilling what you have recognized being your truest heart's wishes and understanding. Place it somewhere in the house where it is in full view, and yet out of the reach of the hands of curious friends and visitors, and of the games of children, perhaps on a mantelpiece, under a glass bell, or behind the glass door of a cupboard. The turquoise will spread its magic throughout the household and will help the happiness of all members of the family, whether they be aware of the magic or not.

induce in you a physical sensation of the desired state. Through this momentary experience you can gather clues and hints on how to change your situation. The herbs will now be connecting you with your home and family environment to show it to you from a space of happiness. From that space, you will be able to see with clarity and compassion what needs doing. As you see, your heart becomes lighter and your head clearer as you breath in and out and feel more at peace, you might see for example the face of your son, and suddenly understand something about your relationship with him which was hindering communication between you. Or you will see a way of having time for some homely pursuits. Or you might

Being Luminous

Health and beauty, grace, elegance, being attractive, all these qualities are really all one and the same thing. And in fact when you are in tune with nature, when you draw from the force and power of existence without hindering yourself in some way, all these qualities, without exception, are yours.

Of course I am not talking here of winning a Miss World contest. Society makes up its own standards of beauty and sexiness which change with its own social and historical structures. Conforming to those standards imparts a certain status of being "beautiful" or "elegant" or "sexy". But this status is dependent on external conditions and has no reality of its own. True beauty, real elegance and grace are beyond societies and cultures, they are external and they alone are not satisfying.

Magic can help you rediscover that beauty in yourself. As it does not depend on any outside factor, or any standard, it is everybody's prerogative. Everybody, no matter what the shape of their nose or length of their legs can be beautiful. In fact they become beautiful when again the life is allowed to flow. Practice with the following incantations and you will soon feel the changes taking place.

If your hair is blond, blond it will stay, unless you dye it; but dying may take out the

Your beauty is uniquely your own — if you do not appreciate it then you will suffer the need to change something which is no more changeable than the beauty of a flower. Good magic, though, can help you understand yourself and the way you need to be.

shine and volume, and you might at one point realize that the true nature of your hair is to crown you like a lion's mane, where before you were trying to make it into a neat casque around your head, and cursed nature for giving you "bad hair".

This can be one of the areas of good magic where the rewards are most apparent and most quick. Have fun!

ALIVENESS MAGIC

Aliveness is the first, and the last, requisite for true beauty and health. This simple magical ritual should at best be performed at the beginning of a weekend, perhaps a Saturday morning, as you will have need of a couple of days during which you are not working. You will need a bloodstone (sanguine jasper), and a little bit of good weather as this is a magic which must be performed outside.

The bloodstone has a strong revitalizing effect; use it even only once and you will have a good feeling of what it is to be alive and well, of feeling the juices of life flowing in your veins, of looking in the mirror and seeing — a truly beautiful you!

This magic needs to be performed during a mild weather season, unless you don't mind the cold so much, because it is performed outside, sitting by the side of a pond or a small river or brook.

Look up on your calendar when the next weekend of waxing moon falls and make plans to have that time relatively free of obligations. It will be fine if family or friends happen to be with you on that weekend, however, as you know, the magic ritual must be performed alone.

That Saturday (or Friday) morning rise early and check the winds with your compass and windsock. If an eastern wind is blowing you can be happy as it is a very good omen. The east wind brings new beginnings, and that is just what you are looking for. However, other winds are not damaging to your purpose. The only thing that might put you off could be rain or snow!

You will have selected a place beforehand. Somewhere peaceful and green. The important part being that if you choose a pond, there should be frogs in it, if you choose a water course, there should be fish. That is necessary to the magic, so make sure that your chosen spot is in fact inhabited!

Take with you a bloodstone, well wrapped

up in a soft cloth, and your cup, and a flask of good wine — if you do not like wine, a few drops (I really mean a few drops) of any other liquor will do (no beer though).

Having reached your place determine the four cardinal points using your compass and mark them with four similar stones. Sit on the water shore, possibly facing east. Place the bloodstone in front of you, and the cup ready with some liquor inside also in front of you.

Relax a while, closing your eyes and feeling your breath going in and out. When you are settled, "complete" yourself, as explained in section one. Feel the balance of the elements within you, and if that balance is somehow unstable redress it by giving more energy to the lacking element.

When you are ready open your eyes and for a while just enjoy the beauty of the morning outside, in the green, the freshness of the water, the sounds of the lapping water on the shore, the birds — any faraway sound of civilization which reaches you there. Smell the air rich with the scent of earth and water and plants and animals. You are already coming closer to nature, closer to yourself.

Now you will let your eyes rest on the water's surface, and without thinking about anything, gently gaze at the water, keeping your look unfocused. Soon, with peripheral vision, you will notice any frog jumping on the stones, if the water is clear, any fish swimming happily below the surface. In this moment the frogs and fish are not ordinary animals. They are your magical allies. If you can clearly distinguish a fish — if a frog jumps up and sits nearly in front of you, seemingly looking at you, you will know that undoubtedly the magic is with you today, and you can ask for anything (within reason) and it will be granted. But if the frogs run away and hide under their stones and leaves, or if you cannot see any sign of fish, if the water is murky or the river bed empty — better try somewhere else, another day.

If the signs are good, continue your magic. First of all call the power water. Then, holding the stone in your left hand, with the right hold the cup to your lips and drink a few sips of the liquid. Feel the warmth of the liquor going down your throat, enlivening your whole being. While you drink ask the bloodstone to shift all hindrances from the natural source of your aliveness, and to make you as fluid as the water in front of you, whose power you have invoked, as vital and innocent as the fish and frogs which have shown you their benevolence and love.

Feel the stone in your hand. If the magic is working the stone will become warmer and you

For lively magic, concerned with the energy of your daily activities, a living pond or river is needed. The river must contain fish or pond frogs or the magic will not carry the living and flowing energy within it.

will feel a tingling sensation spreading from your left arm to the rest of your body. Stay like this for a while, perhaps five to ten minutes, then replace the stone in the sachet and keep it on your body (perhaps tied on a string around your neck). Pour the remaining liquid from the cup onto the ground, and rinse it in the flowing water.

When you are ready you can leave the place, after giving your thanks. Keep the stone on your body during the next two days. In this time, which is a very special time, you must pay close attention to your needs and desires. The magic of the stone is working on you, helping you to release all hindrances to the flow of your own energy.

You might feel like fasting, for example, as your body is willing to release toxins and purify itself — or you might feel like eating mostly yoghurt, fish and spinach, as maybe these alimentations contain what you require to fulfill some internal need. You could feel a strong desire to go for a swim, or a hike in the mountains. Or you might even find yourself irresistibly attracted to your library, and might find new joy and interest in reading or studying. It might be something as seemingly innocent as a wish to go to the movies and have fun for the evening. Whatsoever you truly desire,

Start as the sun rises on the morning before a full moon and your morning ritual will bring pleasure and energy for the whole day.

for these two days, you must follow. (Naturally, only so long as it does not harm anyone — you included).

At the end of the two days, as you go to sleep, again hold the stone in your left hand. Thank it for having guided you in those days, and ask her for a final dream in which you might recognize meaningful messages of your unconscious which will further help your aliveness to come through.

On waking write down the dream in all its details, even if you do not understand its significance. As the changes which you have started within yourself with this magic progress in time, you will be more and more able to decode the meaning of the dream. The day the dream will be totally clear to you, you will be a different person, the magic will have completed its cycle.

SUN MAGIC MORNING RITUAL

Here is a recipe for a morning ritual which, if followed whole-heartedly, will bring not only enhanced appearance and well-being, but will also awaken subtle powers. The ritual is very simple, not many symbols or implements are

required, and anyone can do it. The effect though is strong and reaches deep.

This ritual needs to be effected on mornings preceding a full moon night. You need to start the process as the sun rises, so you will have to get up early. Do not use an alarm clock as the shrillness of the alarm will not help the ritual — do the following instead:

Lie on your back last thing at night and count from ten to zero, visualizing at the same time a huge clock in which the arms are pointing to the time you wish to wake. Then repeat in your mind, without actually speaking: "At this time I will awake." Do this three times and remember to visualize the clock. At the appointed time in the morning you will wake up.

First thing, when you have risen, prepare the following potion:

Take two grams of greek hay (*Trigonella feonum gaecum*) and put it in 100cc of water. Add the peel of the first seasonal fruit which you have eaten that season — you must have kept the peel specially for this occasion. For example you might put aside the peel of the first cherry you ate in summer. Bring the mixture to boil, then let it steep for ten minutes, sweeten with honey and pour it into a porcelain cup.

Greek hay is a powerful herb once used in ancient Egypt, where the priests employed it for religious ceremonies. In Mesopotamia also, it was used together with other herbs in love philters dedicated to the Goddess Astarte. In ancient Greece it was considered the best cure for all cases of physical or mental weakness. The first fruit of the season carries the principles of renewing and rejuvenating life. Drink the potion facing the rising sun and while you drink chant to yourself the following words:

> I rise with thee
> I drink to thee
> Your strength and beauty
> Mine shall be

It is important in this part of the ritual to let the rays of the sun fall on your face and feel the warmth and pleasure on your skin while sipping the potion slowly.

If on the day you chose for this ritual there happens to be a cloudy sky — you are out of luck! You have to start again the next morning, providing there is another one before the moon is full.

This ritual is especially good to follow if you have been ill or tired for some time. The sun so invoked will re-awaken your strength.

WEIGHT LOSS MAGIC PROGRAM

 to

What good would magic be, if it could not provide for one of most women's basic needs, that of losing weight? In fact it is a simple deed to perform, if a bit lengthy — but what are a few days of magic, when sometimes years of efforts, strenuous gymnastics, and suicidal diets have failed!

It might even sound too good to be true — yet true it is. And this you have to believe, as it is the *only* pre-requisite for this magic to work: that unconditionally you believe in it. If you are halfhearted about it, you might as well give up and take up weight-lifting instead.

For this magic you need two things: jasmine essence, and a quartz crystal. Jasmine is the flower of femininity. (I am supposing this magic to be directed to a woman — of course men do want to lose weight too. If this is the case determine from the flower section, or the herb section, which plant would suit you best for this magic). It is the flower of senses, of pleasure, of physical attraction. The best suited therefore to bring you back in touch with the pleasure of being in your skin, of looking and feeling attractive, the feeling that exudes naturally from a healthy and balanced body. In fact all the responsibility for weight problems resides somewhere in the body's loss of its ability to stay balanced. Deficiencies on the emotional or mental plane are interfering with the body's natural wisdom. When its balance is impaired its happiness is lost.

Through jasmine you may magically evoke that lost sensuous joyfulness. With the crystal quartz you focus your energies on the issue at hand, and give staying power to the healing forces.

Begin the process during the day, when the moon is full. Cleanse and dress yourself and sit in your magic place. Place the jasmine flowers or essence and also the quartz crystal in front of you together with the symbols of the elements.

As you call the powers a different element will present itself to you, according to where the imbalance is in you. That will of course change the shape of the incantation. In this example I will use the element air — on the basis of this example you can work out the different variations.

So air is in this case the element which speaks, the power which will help you with this magic. Words belong to air magic. Now inhale the scent of the jasmine and relax deeply to ask your subconscious to give you a word — the key word for this magic. For a few minutes you are sitting with your eyes closed, thinking of nothing. When you sense your mind beginning to wander astray, touch the quartz — its magical powers will help immediately to focus your attention again.

Soon the key word will form itself in your conscious mind: in this example it is "independence". It does not matter that you understand why this particular word should be your key word. Certainly a reason is there, your unconscious has its own deep wisdom — but it is not important that you should be consciously aware of its motives.

Every night, from the full moon to the black moon, you will rub a few drops of jasmine oil on your naked body. While doing this, let the key word "independence" stay in your mind.

As you revel in the fragrance of the jasmine, relaxing, images will come to your mind, suggestions as to how to expand on the independence in your life. Maybe you will have a vision of yourself learning a foreign language. Following these suggestions is an essential part of this magic; if you want it to work you will have to find a way.

The quartz will help you with that. If you find yourself saying "I have too much to do, I

Lavender washes away old attitudes and guilts, acting on your soul to clean you of rubbish — like a magical soap.

cannot possibly fit this in, I never was good at languages anyway," etc., touch the crystal and feel its energy for a few seconds. It will immediately give you clarity and firmness of purpose, and you will be able to see what you need to do, and have the determination to do it.

Every night, before going to sleep, rub the essence on your body, and experiment with your key word. Keep the crystal with you at all times for this period — to touch it whenever you feel that you need to do so.

Thanks to the magic of the flower, of the crystal, and of the key word given to you by the power air, a deep change will start in this period. A change which will enable you to regain your natural balance, and the grace and beauty that go with it.

LAVENDER GUILT BANISHING INCANTATION

From part two (if you have not read it go to it now) you will know about lavender and its properties. Lavender acts on your soul as a kind of magical soap, washing away all clouds of old attitudes, all cobwebs of thoughts of guilt. The following is a good incantation to perform when you are feeling the need of a magical cleaning.

It is best, on this occasion, to wait for the midnight hour, in a night of waning moon. If you cannot wait until that time (perhaps you must rise early to go to work) then any time between nine p.m. and midnight will do. Midnight is the time for banishing magic — and that is your purpose, to banish old, unthwarted feelings of guilt, of shame, of self-denial. The waning moon also exercises the power of decreasing the energy — when you expose some part of your heart to a waning moon, that part will loose its grip on you, and soon will disappear altogether — like the moon.

If a north or a west wind are blowing on your appointed night it is a very good sign, as these winds are of great help to this particular magic. For this incantation you need to have the lavender oil at your disposal, prepared as it is described in part two.

Also, if your ill-ease reflects itself on your physical appearance; that is if you look in the mirror and you see yourself as ugly even though you might know that there is nothing wrong with your looks, you will prepare a decoction of the root of burdock to use in your magic in conjunction with the oil of lavender. The burdock has the property of cleansing your

physical space of negative feelings. Together with the lavender oil, which acts on your heart space, the process will be doubly as powerful.

On that evening do not overload your stomach with food: eat light and early. When you have finished your activities for the day, find some space for yourself alone, and relax a while: maybe read a good book — go for a walk if the surroundings are safe and pleasant, play on an instrument if you know one, or just listen to a relaxing musical piece. When the appointed time comes, cleanse and dress yourself and enter your magic space, taking there with you the root decoction and the lavender oil.

Extinguish all electric lights, and let only the candles and the flames from your burner light your actions. Before proceeding with the Calling the Powers ritual, look outside your window to find the gentle waning moon. Recommend yourself to her with some simple words which might come to you in this moment.

As you then call the powers of the elements and come to hold the purpose of your magic in mind, visualize the feelings you wish to banish. See them as dark clouds surrounding you, let the dark clouds just be there around you, without being upset by them.

Let us say that, for our example, the element

Dreams should be recorded when magic is practised — they will indicate necessary changes to your life and influence the next magic you plan to do.

which will answer you this time, is earth. From this you can understand that what is producing your negative feelings is a lack of earth, a lack of grounding — because your connection with earth is poor, your insecurity takes the faces of unresolved guilt and self-chastisement. This happens often; when a person's ability to draw nourishment and security from the surroundings is impaired, the resulting low energy takes the form of fear and negative patterns. It is then to earth that you must address yourself — to the warm, embracing mother who is always ready to offer rest and food.

Mix a few drops of the lavender oil to the burdock root decoction, take some paste in your hand and distribute it evenly over your face, as you would a face mask. (The ingredients used in the root decoction and lavender oil are beautifying for the skin).

As you do this imagine that you are lying your body to rest in a mound of soft, humid, dark earth. Feel the wetness on your face, and know it to be the womb of the great mother Earth. In your mind repeat these words:

I come back to you earth
take the poison out
and leave me clean.

Lie down and relax more and more, descending into yourself. While doing that you see the dark clouds which were representing your negative feelings descend into the ground and be re-absorbed by earth.

When the clouds are all gone, rinse your face of the paste with water, and dry yourself gently. Then look at your luminous self in your magic mirror and rejoice in the beautiful person that is you.

Make a note of the dreams which will come to you that night, as they will be no ordinary dreams. They will contain indications from the power earth of ways in which you can improve your grounding. For example, if you would dream of climbing a mountain, it could mean that you need a worthier challenge in your life. Or maybe you would dream of a wallet full of money. Earth is telling you that you must take more care of the financial side of things.

Be open to the meaning of your dreams in that night. It is earth speaking to you.

BEING CHARMING FOR ONE NIGHT

There will always be an occasion when you

want to be truly irresistible — especially if you are a woman. Although I have said over and over again that magic is not to be used to trifle with, I think that, in this case, it is not terrible to cheat a little bit. I doubt that even the gods of magic will frown on you for this — why would they have given witch hazel the magical powers of granting irresistible attractiveness for a few hours to the wise users, if they did not want to have it that way?

This is a ritual to perform in the privacy of your own bathroom. It can be done anytime of day or night, no matter what is the phase of the moon and what incredible winds are blowing.

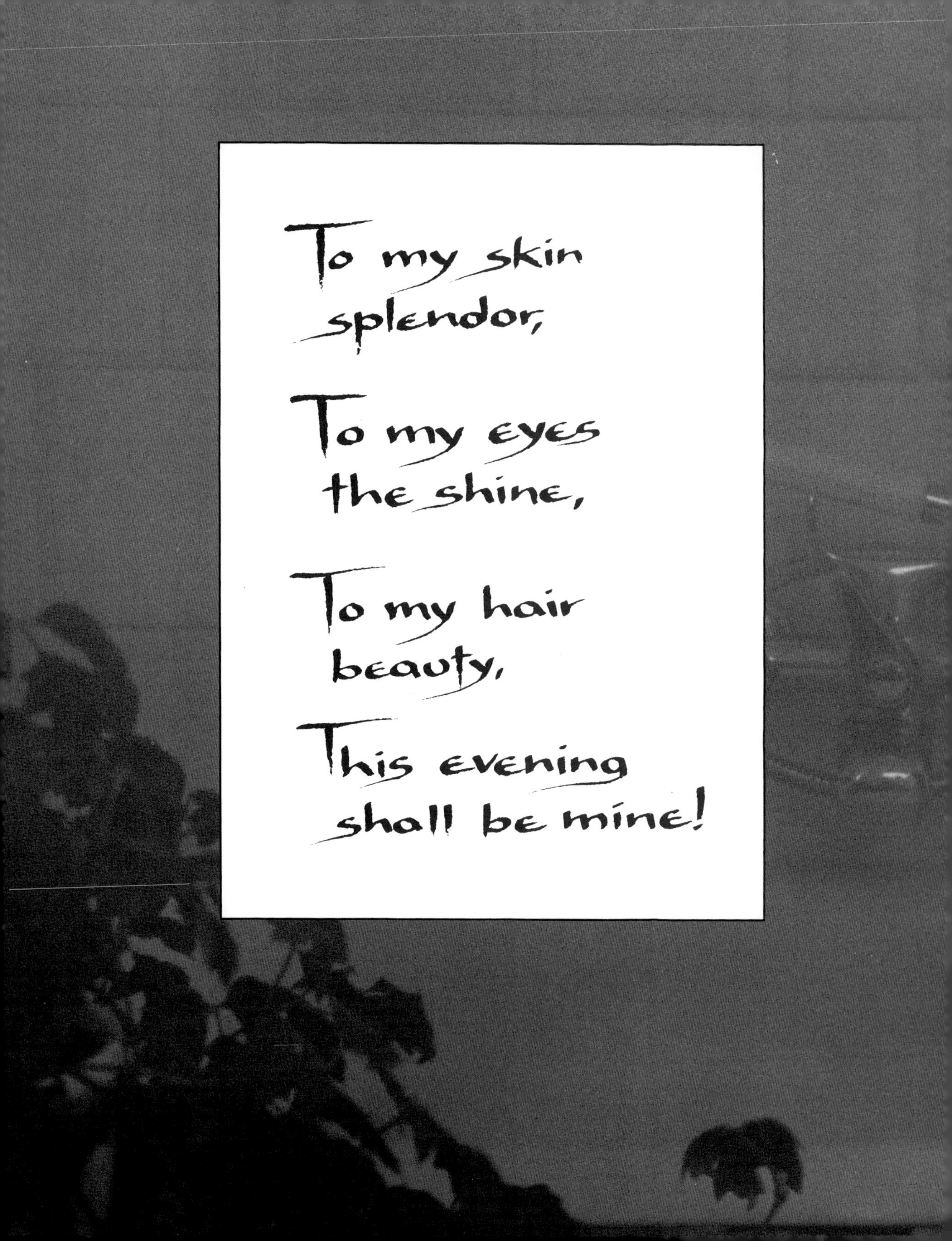

To my skin
splendor,

To my eyes
the shine,

To my hair
beauty,

This evening
shall be mine!

All you need is the time to take a bath and your magic herb, either grown by yourself or purchased and consecrated. Only one thing you must remember: this incantation will not work if you perform it more than once in a moon cycle.

Prepare a few leaves of witch hazel in a bowl and keep it by the side of the bath. Prepare your bath water as you would for any normal bath. Extinguish all electric light and leave only the flames of one or more candles burning, to your preference. If you wish, you might have an incense burning, possibly a light and sweet smelling one. When you are ready to enter the water take the bowl with the herb, empty it in the bath water and say the words on page 214. If you perform your magic for a daytime occasion, just change the word "evening" for whatever your requirement might be.

Lie in the water and feel the magic working on you. See yourself as a true goddess in the situation you are preparing for. Imagine the whole scene from your point of view, only you are a queen, an empress, a goddess of beauty and grace. See what you are wearing, how you move and speak, who you connect with, and with what feelings and expectations.

Be careful, as you might have some surprises. Maybe you are normally a very talkative person, and you the "goddess" just sits beautifully and observes her surroundings without bothering to participate in conversations she does not really have any interest in. Perhaps you are normally very shy, while the new you has no trouble at all directing all her energy towards the people in the party she really likes and wishes to get acquainted with.

This is really an exercise to get you acquainted with what will happen in the next few hours. Otherwise the shock of being, suddenly, as attractive as a real goddess might be a little too much to bear, and you might end up spoiling everything by starting to cry or to laugh, where you are supposed to talk reasonably.

Of course, when you use the witch hazel, you must be aware that *all* the men will be attracted to you (or *all* the women as the case might be), and you need to know how to fend off unacceptable suitors and how to behave in front of the bewitched men's wives and girlfriends.

It is true, things might get out of control — and being under the influence of an incantation, there will be nothing you can do about it. I recommend you take a really good friend along with you. And it must be *really* a good friend, because I myself know of no one who would not become jealous herself, and leave me to my destiny!

CAMELLIA RITUAL

Your bathroom will this morning be adorned by a single camellia, which is the flower of unpretending excellence. It will give you the quality of beauty without pretension; of pure and simple elegance. You will also have ready the following essences for your bath: cypress, lavender and lemon. Mix two drops of each into the bath water. Light a candle, a red one if you are married or otherwise involved with a partner; or a white one if you are single and wish to remain so. Place it next to the camellia so that both the candle and the flower are easily visible from where you will be lying in the bath. Have within easy reach some red clay, or an oil of your liking.

First lie in the bath and relax deeply, counting from ten to zero. Once you have reached a quiet, comfortable state, open your eyes and gently gaze at the flame of the candle. The white flower will be in your field of vision but you should not look at it directly as this would change your vibrations and spoil the incantation. After a few minutes sit upright, without changing your scope of vision — reach for the clay or oil pot, and dip the index finger of your left hand into it. With enough paste to make a sign, draw a cross just below your navel, saying:

Essence of camellia, enter me.

Then another cross between your breasts, again saying:

Essence of camellia, enter me.

Finally one on your forehead, this time very slowly, still without looking directly at the flower. Imagine that it grows bigger and bigger until it fills the whole room saying:

Essence of camellia, stay with me.

Rinse out the clay or oil before leaving the bath. Repeat the ritual three times on the mornings following three consecutive full moons. With this your face and body will assume the quiet elegant beauty of the camellia.

Works of Magic

Magic is nowhere needed as much as in the everyday work of daily life. Where normal answers might fail and frustration set in, a simple incantation, a quick call to nature's magical allies, can resolve a situation and bring you more than a step forward. And if you really have only time left for sleeping, and no more — you can try a dream magic — as you can follow in the example below.

DREAM TO WORK MAGIC

Using dreams is one of the best ways of performing magic, specially for a lazy person. You have to do very little, as everything happens while you sleep. This incantation is related to a working matter — but the same method can be applied to any other issue in your life, from love to money to health. In this example you want to find a job, and you would like magic to help you on your way.

In the evening (for this magic no special timing requirement is necessary) before going to sleep cleanse and dress yourself, and sit in your magic space for a few minutes. Take there with you an infusion of valerian (the herb which helps dream-magic) and the fluorite

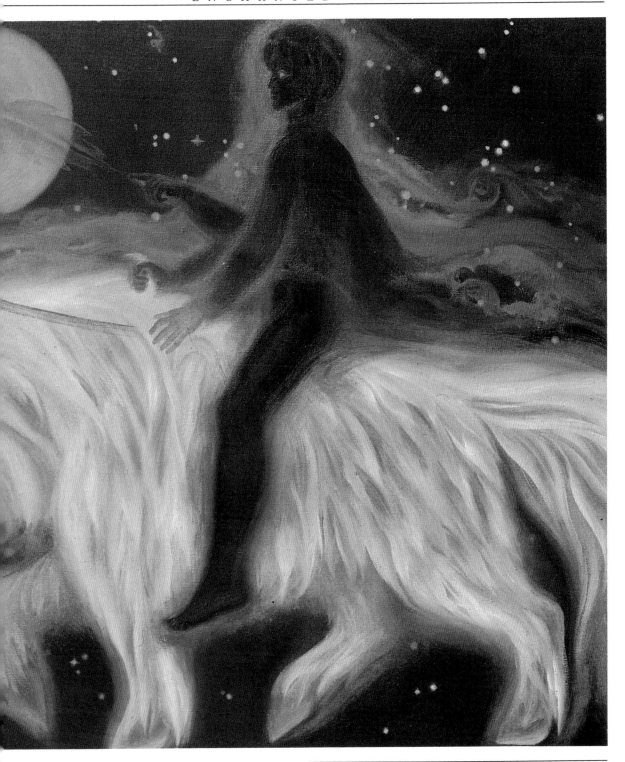

Previous page
Dreams can be enhanced and even brought about by the use of the correct herbs and potions. Follow the method on this page and you will see how to enter your own dreams.

octahedron, the stone of work. After having completed yourself drink the infusion holding the cup with one hand, while in the other hand you still hold the magic stone. While you are doing that imagine yourself at your favorite work and feeling very happy at it. Then say these words:

This is valerian,
to take me to the land
of dreams.
This is the stone,
to make the dream
come true.

As you then go to bed, while you are falling asleep, make sure your mind does not wonder from the subject of finding a job. That does not mean that you need to sit there worrying about it. Just keep the image in your mind of yourself performing a happy task, one you would be glad to have as yours. Keep this visualization light and serene, add details to it if you want: you could see your surroundings, you can imagine yourself going to and from work. The fluorite octahedron will stay this night under your

pillow. As the *very last thing* in your mind before you fall asleep, formulate your request to the stone:

To you stone I speak
grant me the wish
this work to find.

As you know, the words don't have to be exactly those. Any way of saying the same thing, if you really feel it, will be fine. But remember, though it might be difficult, these have to be the very last words you pronounce in your mind before falling asleep. If your mind should happen to wander off on other subjects, the magic will not work. If you do everything right, in the night you will have a dream which will clearly indicate to you the way to your new job. Perhaps you will not even remember the dream, but nevertheless the instruction will be there, and unconsciously you will be carrying it through.

Perhaps you will dream of a forgotten friend, who suddenly calls you up just to say hello. This friend has a present for you. A few days later, when by chance you meet an acquaintance you will suddenly remember your dream — and without even consciously thinking about it you will be telling this person about your hopes for such and such work. A few days later the same person will be calling you to tell you of an opening which they have come to know about...

Be open to the ways of magic, for magic always finds you when you call!

KNOWING WHAT YOU WANT TO DO

There are always times in your life when you reach a crossroad. You must decide which direction to take next and the importance of the decision might be enough to cloud your mind. One such time could be at the moment of leaving school, where you must decide whether to continue studying or join the working world. Another time might be when you are offered a promotion which involves a change of work and residence, or on the occasion that you have just lost a job: you might take the opportunity to see if you want to continue on the same road, or if you need to change. The situations are many.

The following magic will be of great help to you in such a moment — it will give you a deep insight into what you really need and want to do. A sound decision in a critical moment can save you from years of misery and wasted efforts! This magic is special, as it involves isolating oneself in nature. It depends on you, and on your experiences in nature as to what degree you want to take this adventure. The magic itself only needs a short time; maybe a couple of hours, between finding a congenial spot, relaxing and concentrating, and performing the appropriate actions. But if you can stay away for a whole day, or even better a day and a night, and perform the magic after you have spent hours in solitude and relaxation in contact with nature — it will be of course all the more powerful an experience.

The hour to perform the magic must be sunset, and you must be, as I have said, in an isolated spot in nature. But do not put yourself at risk by going to some dangerous place. If you are afraid, go with a friend, and ask him or her to stay within hearing distance of you while you perform your magic.

With four stones and a compass determine the four cardinal points, and sit facing east, the place of new beginnings. You will have taken with you some jimson weed, the magic herb to give you insight into your deepest wishes. If you are not familiar with building outside bonfires, also take your own little iron burner:

Magic is needed at all times — not only in the privacy of troubled times or in happiness and love but also in normal working hours and during those times that seem to be just routine. Magic will change the routine.

the one you use to invoke the elements. Once you have got the fire going, take a pinch of the herb and throw it into the fire. In the flames you will now see what your truest wishes are. Don't be surprised if they are very different from what you thought they would be! The longer you will have been outside, by yourself in touch with nature, the clearer will be the images in the flames for you to read.

ABUNDANCE MAGIC

This magic is very simple, and should really be performed by everyone. It opens you to abundance, to wealth, to being comfortable and well taken care of. There really is no reason at all to be poor and miserable in this world (unless, of course, you like to live very simply — and there is a certain beauty in that, too), as it is simple to feel the abundance of existence, and to make that happen in your own life.

Find an agate with fossils, the stone of richness, and get some basil seeds. Wait for a new moon night, when the wind is blowing from the east. For this magic the east wind, of changes and new beginnings, is essential. It is worthwhile waiting for a few days, if that is the

case — this is certainly an incantation you would not want to go wrong! As soon as the right wind is blowing, take your stone, and the seeds, and go to your magic garden. Or take a

pot, and some earth if you have an indoor spot. Facing the direction of the wind proceed to plant the seeds in the earth. Place the stone next to the seeds, deep in the earth, but not so close to the seeds that they are hindered in their growth. As your plant will grow, so will your wealth.

FINDING YOUR OWN POWER

This should be one of the most important lessons in the growing-up process: one day the child realizes that he has a right to his own code of behavior, to his own truth. What his parents (the authority figures of childhood) say no longer represents inviolable law, but merely suggestions of older people — sometimes wise, sometimes not. Instead what most often happens is that a person is never helped to reach that point of self-sufficience, neither by his parents, nor by society. After leaving the original family the young man or woman will be, consciously or unconsciously looking for another authority figure to replace the one he or she has just left. Sure enough it will be found — in the boss at work, or even in the husband or wife, or in a so-called friend, or in some cases in an ideology or religious sect. Such a situation will poison the life of a person. No freedom is possible in it, no real responsibility is exercised.

If you should become aware that this is the

We very often go through our whole lives without finding our own individual sense of authority and power — another matter that magic can help. Good magic for good power.

case with you, or if a friend should need your help in this situation, remember the magic gifts of the tiger's eye. This beautiful stone is the best gift possible to adolescents in the process of becoming adults. It helps the process of adulthood to happen freely and healthily, without traumas, and without other hindrances. When otherwise used in magic, the tiger's eye gives strength and self-confidence. Its powers re-inforce self-esteem, and make it possible to assert one's own individuality in a free and mature way, in harmony with nature and with other people. Tiger's eye is best used in conjunction with the power fire.

Make yourself ready for magic, "complete" yourself, and call fire. You will have the stone ready by you so that after calling the power you can take it in your left hand and hold it close to the flames of the burner, so that the warm light of fire can shine on the stone, and heat up its spirit and magic. Pronounce your wish, speaking it aloud in a strong and clear voice. (While in most incantations the words are pronounced softly, in this one it is required to speak up loud and clear). You might want to say something very simple like:

Give me the strength and clarity

To be myself and to stand by myself.

Or make up your own rhymes for a long spell. For the tiger's eye incantation it is above all required that you find your own way to express what you need and want. It can be the simplest or the most complicated way of expressing it, as long as it is your own.

Then write your words on the appropriate paper, light two candles, a red and a black one (the black symbolizing the death of the old, the red the flame of strength and courage), and leave them burning for three days and three nights. If you know your candle will not last the night you have two choices: buy a thicker candle, or set the alarm clock to wake up in time to change the candle. As in all candle magic you must *not* let the flames die until the end of the prescribed time, or the magic will be spoiled. During this time the tiger's eye will rest in the proper spell box, laying over it the paper on which you have written your wishes.

After the three nights you might remove the stone and extinguish the candles — but it is a good idea to wear the stone, either in a ring or a pendant until you feel you have reached firm ground within your own standing.

Worlds of Shadows

I am sure there will be many among you who want to know about ghosts and visions, death and after death — about talking with spirits and anything else that might be unexplainable and unfathomable. We might call these the worlds of shadows, as their existence is as vague and as cool as that of shadows who mix and merge within each other — yet remain unbreakable and invincible in their own light.

INITIATION TO THE OTHER WORLD

The first thing to remember is that just as everyone has his own subjective view of the material world, so everyone has to experience different dimensions of reality in his own particular way; a way that is unforeseeable and unpredictable. In fact the differences between individual experiences of other dimensions is much stronger than the difference in perceptions of the material world. These dimensions, in their consistency, are much more alike to that quality of the mind we call imagination. Obviously there can be no guidelines as to what to expect. And to know about what has happened to other people is of course interest-

ing but only as it is interesting to read someone else's love story.

What follows now is a device to put you in that space from where the experience is possible. It is a difficult trick. And not many of those who are curious are also courageous. The essential and foremost requirement is to really want access to these different dimensions. One must be totally, completely positive about that desire. It is a good sign when it feels almost as if the desire were there in spite of oneself. If one feels drawn, compelled to look, even if at the same time telling oneself that this is totally insane — this is an indication of readiness.

At this point, by far the easiest thing to do is to choose a place where the vibrations are already eerie. A house, a castle, a dark countryside road crossing or even an empty room in a deserted house. Find one such place convenient to you — and wait for the next full moon night. Don't go there on a full stomach, or having had too much to drink — and possibly avoid smoking for that evening. Your clothes should be plain, and dark of color. Be sure that you are not wearing a heavy belt as that would break the flow of energy in your body, which now needs to be easy and unhindered. And you must go alone!

There is a place inside everybody where all

voices come to rest — a twilight zone of silence, where passions forget themselves: a place the scientists call the "alpha" state of mind. That state is the borderline. That's where you want to reach.

After you are in the location you have chosen, at the right time, everything should be dark except for the moonlight, lie down on the floor or ground and close your eyes. (If it is cold, lay a blanket down, or lie on a bench). It is likely that you'll be afraid: alone, in the dark, in a deserted place, very likely a haunted one, at an ungodly hour of the night, and waiting for ghosts to appear! In fact, if you are afraid it simply means that you are receptive and your energy is high, and that the vibrations of the place are playing on you. The fear is your mind in its "ready to go" state, all bells ringing, all lights flashing — as far from "alpha" state as you could possibly be. But just for that reason, by the law of opposites, the higher your fear, the deeper the state of relaxation you can reach if you manage to bypass it.

So there you are lying on the ground in darkness. Imagine a big sphere hovering above you. In that sphere you pack all your fears, your passions, your ideas, all people who are attached to you and whom you are attached to. The sphere is tied to you with a silver cord, which you will imagine yourself breaking with the index and middle finger of your left hand. Some strange experiences can happen with this method. You might see in the sphere wild faces contorting and screaming, mouths shouting in anguish. Or you might see strange symbols or geometrical figures — the sphere might seem to expand more and more, threatening to engulf you.

You are putting your identity in that sphere, and there are facets of it which you are not aware of. So angry, passionate people, whose emotions are hot, are likely to see their heat in the sphere, and might find it bursting into flames above their eyes. On the other hand the coldness of the methodical, calculating personalities might project itself as an image of an icy ring inside the sphere. And if there is one particular thing disturbing you in this moment of your life, it will certainly appear inside your sphere, if you are doing things right. It could be

Previous page and left
Good magic can also enter the realms of ghosts and doubts! Here the dimensions touch one another and overlap but a book of magic would not be complete without some words on the darker side, even if the darkness is of the soft variety.

a person, a situation, even just an idea. It could be either plain and clear — perhaps someone's face; or a symbol, a rising sun for example, if you are expecting a new job.

Don't try to understand those images, let them float there in the sphere above you. Let them do what they want, and change as much as they like. A point will come when the activity inside the sphere begins to subside, and you will feel ready to cut the cord. Only these two things you *must* remember: whatever images might have come up, make sure they stay *inside* the sphere. If the image is outside in some way, put it back in. If you cannot do that for some reason, it is better to stop the experience. You don't have sufficient awareness and control over yourself and a meeting with unfamiliar presences might be actually harmful.

The second thing to remember when you are about to cut the cord is that the experience is totally yours. It is *your* sphere, created by your imagination, you are its master, and it is you who is deciding to set it free. Once it is free all your fear will be gone and you will find yourself, alone, on the borderline; that is the confine between the levels of existence we are familiar with and the ones we are not. Not everybody will want to cross that borderline.

Those who do will be stepping into the world of pure magic.

MAKING FRIENDS WITH THE FULL MOON

If you are one of those people who become always edgy and impossible when the time of the full moon comes, but, on the other hand, also feel like you would really like to learn to use its power — try following these suggestions.

Starting with the first quarter of the moon, find yourself a moonstone (can be a ring, some earrings, a pendant — or even just a lose stone which you will carry around in a small soft pouch, on your body) and wear it, day and night, until the moon comes to full. The moonstone alone will be working on your subtle energies putting you in harmony with the energy of the moon. It is likely that during this period of influence of the moonstone you will notice some strange things about yourself.

Perhaps you have always been a gregarious person, liking big companies of friends with lots of fun and laughter — and now suddenly you find yourself spending more and more time on your own. Perhaps you have always liked a

Some people feel uncomfortable and edgy at the night of the full moon — women are particularly prone to ill emotions at this time. But it is possible to become friends with this glorious world in the sky.

certain kind of music, and now you find a curiosity and an interest growing for a different one. Indulge these new developments of your personalities as much as you can — you can only be enriched by discovering a different side to yourself.

As the moon grows and is approaching its fullness, take a little time out each evening, perhaps just before going to bed, to make yourself an infusion of camomile (or if you don't like the taste of it, choose another herb from the herb chart) and to sit under the sky, either in the garden or balcony, or open window, absorbing the light of the moon. You are not to do anything — no words to repeat, no actions to perform. Just sit there under the moon, and let her embrace you in her cool silvery scent. Just for a few minutes, for at least a week before the full moon, do nothing but be with her every night. By the time the moon is full again, you will be ready to welcome her power, and to use it in your magical practices.

CONNECTING WITH YOUR GUIDING SPIRIT

The notion of a "spirit guide" is a very old one:

it is sufficient to think of the "guardian angel" of the Catholic faith. A spirit guide is an entity which accompanies you throughout your life, looking after you and your spiritual development. Whether this entity is the soul of someone you knew in a "past life" and who is now still unborn and for love and compassion wants to lend you a hand (a wing?), or whether it is something totally alien to your way of being — this is not for me to say, the experience is personal and so is the truth of it.

If you really wish to make the experience, magic can help you. The stones to use are the opal and the moonstone. The herb is the hellebore which will open you to the mysterious worlds of the spirits (as this herb is poisonous great care must be taken to use it properly and to not absorb it). Wait for the next full moon night.

This magic must be performed at midnight, so you must manage somehow to wait till this hour. Choose a room, or a place outside, or on your balcony from where the full moon is in plain view.

If by any chance the sky should be clouded and hide the moon from your view, the incantation cannot take place — as that would be a sure sign that the spirit world does not want to reveal itself to you.

There are so many stories about fairies; stories of their presence in secret places, seen only by children and adepts of magic. But the simplest way to feel the presence of such spirits is in the form of guides that are there to aid your progress to happiness. You may never actually see them in your own reality but you can always find their feeling close to your heart.

To say "spirit world" is rather a vague expression, I grant. But whatever that might mean to you of one thing you must always be sure, so to avoid useless fears: the "spirit world" is wise and compassionate — it will not reveal itself to you if you are not ready for it. Everything in existence, spirit or not spirit, will treat you with care and intelligence if you are sincerely seeking to better yourself and to grow in understanding and love.

Of course, if your intents are stupid, as for example, if you are trying to prove yourself powerful by calling up the spirits, existence might just want to teach you a lesson, and you could end up being scared stiff. But you will have called that upon yourself, and should blame only yourself for it.

To go back to our incantation, if the moon should be covered by clouds do not attempt any further magic, and let a few months pass before you think again of this magic. But if the moon shines beautifully on you, making your magic stones like liquid stars in front of you — and even better, if a north wind blows at that time, you can safely go ahead.

Sit in front of the symbols of the elements, having readied yourself, with only the moonlight to enlighten your activities. On one side there will be a bowl with a few leaves of hellebore and vervain mixed in it. The magic stones, the opal and the moonstone, will shine in front of you, laying on a piece of black velvet.

Call the power air, then take a pinch of the mixed herbs, grind it between your fingers, and shake it loose in the wind. As you do that connect in your heart with your spirit guide, and say the words on page 234. Carefully rinse your hands with the water contained in the cup, dry them on the velvet cloth, then take up the stones, lie down where you are and place them on your heart.

Close your eyes and only follow the rhythm of your breath, imagine your breath to be the waves of the sea gently breaking on the shore, one following the other, one merging into the other. As you so dissolve in the gentle rhythm of the night, if you are ready, your spirit guide will show itself to you. It will probably be in the form of a vision that will present itself with blinding clarity to your soothed mind. It could be just a face, or a form, or... it is not for me to know, or to say. Such a meeting can be a very sweet and happy event, and certainly an important one. Once seen so clearly the presence of a being which is there just for you, helping you, will give you such a feeling of "having a friend" that will stay forever.

If in your wisdom
The time has come
And mine and your heart
In truth are one
Through moonstone and opal
And moon's magic light
Come here to seek me
This long sweet night.

Future Now

Tell me my future! That could be a full time occupation for every gypsy, witch or magician who had the time and inclination. Everybody, at least sometimes, is interested to know what is going to happen tomorrow, and how this particular situation will resolve itself, and will my lover leave me or marry me, and so on and so forth.

The greater part of the interest in magic is always dominated by a desire of knowing the unknowable — the future — of controlling the uncontrollable, that which has not happened yet. Yet the thing in itself is so simple that many of us truly wonder how the whole misunderstanding came about. Because a misunderstanding it is. The future has not happened and you cannot know it — there is nothing more to it than that. The present is happening now, and that you can know, in fact you should know, and know it much better than you do.

As your understanding of the present deepens you will see how you are creating this very moment your future, every part of it. Then not only can you "tell" what is going to happen, but you can also change it.

As things stand now, for the greater part, a few clever and unscrupulous people just make money out of reading the signs which you

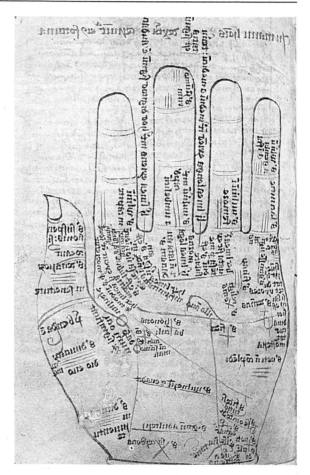

yourself give out of how you are constructing your own future, and then they give them back to you, as something out of your power: "It is in the stars that you will be married three

Previous page
Fortune telling is different from magic but also part of it — the difference is mainly our misunderstanding of how it works. We think in the future while magic acts in the present.

Left
Try the divination on these pages and you may see how your own determination makes that future you wish to see into.

times." All there is, is a predisposition in you perhaps to be unstable in your relationship. Looked at it this way there is a lot you can do about it. If you leave it up to the stars to find you three husbands, nothing ever is going to change in your life.

DIVINATION RITUAL

To be able to see into the future has always been one of man's greatest desires. Great sums of money are paid all over the world just to know some irrelevant detail of one's own life to come. Why this madness? What does it matter now to know what will happen tomorrow? It gives a momentary feeling of security. Because you know you are to some extent in control of the situation. Yet, when man is in closer contact to his own magic potential, he can see that control over outside events is in fact not needed at all, as it is he himself who creates his own reality.

In this context divination acquires a totally different meaning. As in all good magic the principle of it is to go back to the roots of yourself, where you are already busy creating that very future you are so curious about. The following is one method of divination which is very ancient yet very little known. Try it and you will not only see your future, but you will also have a direct experience of yourself determining it.

As you will know from the chapter on the four elements, one of the ways of doing water magic, is well magic. Well magic brings you to the depths of your being, and it is certainly a good method to use on this occasion. It might require a trip to the countryside, but you need to provide for this magic a flask of real well water — it needs to be fresh and drinkable (even though you will not be drinking it), because if the well is in disuse and the water stagnant the magic would not be flowing in it. Have ready also a small amount of dried powdered henbane, as this is the herb to expand your faculties of clairvoyance.

This magic must be performed at night — any time after the sun has set, in a time of waxing moon. Prepare two bowls of the same size and shape and pour in each one of them some of the well water. Add to the first bowl enough red ink to color the water a deep red color. Add to the second bowl the same amount of blue ink to render that water blue. Light your burner, and throw a pinch of henbane in the flames saying:

Tarot is one of the most ancient and beautiful forms of divination, but do not get caught in the idea that the future is somehow set and you can always predict the truth — this is not how it works. In fact you will always get the opposite of what you definitely predict because fate does not appreciate definites.

With henbane it shall be that my future I'll see.

Now place the two bowls in front of you at a such a distance so that you can comfortably see them both. Fix your sight on a point in the middle of the bowls, crossing slightly your eyes as you do so. (This will not be harmful to your eyes). At first you will probably have four bowls in your visual field. If you relax more and keep on looking, the two in the middle will completely superimpose each other, and you will have three bowls in your field. The red, the blue, and the middle one which is both blue and red. If you relax deeper still, there will come a moment when the two outside bowls will disappear, and only the middle one will remain.

In that moment you will be able to see your future in the well water. What you will see probably will be a shock to you, and you are likely to jump and loose your focus. Don't get upset — just start again. In fact what you are going to see is yourself.

Perhaps your question was about work. You wanted to know if the promotion you had been waiting for was forthcoming. What you will see in the magic well water, is your own entire truth about the situation. You will see the most superficial layer of yourself wanting the promotion. You will see perhaps another layer opposing that idea, feeling unworthy of it, and then yet another layer of yourself knowing that this promotion must happen as it is necessary to continue your growth in life. You will then see exactly how many difficulties you will put on your path to reach this promotion (as that layer in you feels you are not worth it), and you will see when and how you will finally let yourself obtain it. This will all happen in the space of seconds, and it will hit you as a lightning of understanding, in the exact moment the two bowls of magic water become one, sharp and clear, in your visual field.

After this revelation you might want to work on the layers of yourself which are making life hard for you. You could perhaps do a guilt-banishing magic. Or perhaps simply find a friend and expose your fears and negative attitudes to him or her. Just talking about it will help you see ways of getting them out of the way. Anyway this divination method, when successful, is quite a powerful experience. Remember though, it will only reveal truths regarding yourself and the way you relate to other people — and what is going to happen following those patterns. The patterns can be changed though!

Water connects with the unconscious and must be found outside for the purpose of water scrying. This takes the diviner into wide open spaces and a new experience in magic.

TAROT FOR DIVINATION

Through the tarot cards you can explore the patterns and reveal the future of others as well as your own. The tarot cards pulled by the person you are doing a session for will reveal the layers acting in that person and the probable outcome from the interplay of those layers. As a reader you can suggest the person you are reading the cards to, ways of freeing himself/herself of the restrictive, destructive layers of the personality in order to reach to happier future potential.

Don't get caught in the trap of seeing the future as a set thing which you can in some ways reveal, perhaps to gain fame and money: this is one of the worst ways of misusing magic, and the sad thing is that this is exactly what is happening a lot today. Some people at the threshold of magic get enchanted with what they can see and to suit their own purposes make that into a definite reality, and then proceed to exploit it. Follow these instructions when giving yourself or others a tarot reading and you will transform it into a truly magical experience.

Let yourself and the person you are giving a reading to relax together for a few minutes. Light a candle and let both of you gaze softly at the flame (it is best if the rest of the room is in darkness). You will have prepared an infusion of anise, thyme and camomile — whose magical properties will together open the subtler levels of your energy, and will help you see into the other person's heart. Drink it together. Then let the inquirer shuffle the cards until he feels it is enough. Spread the cards out onto a special cloth which you keep solely for this purpose. A black velvet, or red, is good — but any other will do, preferably of one color. Keep together with your cards the stone amethyst, which favors a meditative state, and the aquamarine, for clear thinking. Before starting the reading, silently complete yourself, so that you are whole and calm. Then tune in with the other person's energy, perhaps by holding his or her hands — and ask him to draw a card.

The seed of the card (whether swords-air, wands-fire, cups-water, pentacles-earth) will tell you which element dominates the reading for this person. So if the card is one of swords, you will know that you are dealing in the world

of air; thoughts, communication, ideas, words. It is in this rarefied world that you will find a path to understand and help your friend.

After the inquirer has chosen the decided number of cards, and you have interpreted them (for detailed study of tarot consult one of the many books on the market), put out the candle, and thank the power air.

WATER SCRYING

Water scrying outside in nature is one of the softest and nicest methods of divination. If moreover you own an emerald and can take it with you when attempting to reach the deeper levels of the unconscious, success will be assured.

Leave home early in the morning, and go by the side of a river, or lake, or other watercourse. The sunlight must shine on the water, but not so directly that it glares. Take your emerald and dip it into the water. While you look at it, its reflection dancing under the surface, ask it to help you, by shining its magic light into the darkest corners of your unconscious mind. Then take it out and hold it in your left hand as you let your eyes gaze at the surface of the water, unfocused. Your look must be soft, and your eyes half closed. You are seeing, but not looking at anything in particular. It is a bit like you are letting the water look at you, rather than you looking at the water.

Hold the question in your mind for a few moments let it fill your mind and your being totally, while you stay relaxed, and keep on gazing at the water.

Then let the question go, and let your mind be empty. As you gaze, you will see images on the water surface. These images will be as clear to you as words written in a book, and will tell you all you want to know. You might be asking about a forthcoming voyage. Will it be successful? What is the importance and meaning of this trip in your life? Etc.

As you scry the water, you might see a child growing up to become an adult. Or a bird growing very strong wings and flying away... The art of scrying is a very beautiful ancient one. Not everyone though is gifted for this art. If the ripples and waves of the water surface remain silent for you, it is better to choose another method of divination.

Epilogue

Probably quite some time has passed since you first picked up this book. In the course of reading it and experiencing it, you will have come to see many things in a different light.

If even a small part of good magic has entered your life, it is going to be there to stay, and it will grow — whether you notice it or not. Soon one morning, pouring tea, just by the way the liquid gathers in the cup you will be able to tell what kind of day you are going to have; or if a friend comes to you with trouble... just by looking at him or her you will know what the trouble is really all about and what is the best way to help.

Keep in your heart only this one golden rule, and all else will follow: *cherish existence and what it makes available.* Look around to find out what makes you smile inside: flowers, seashells, birds and fishes, people or sounds or colors... it can be any or all of it! Treasure it, care for it, give it time and energy; look at it, play with it, talk to it, feel it, smell it, touch it — become friends and cherish that friendship. This is your magic tool and through that tool it is easy to enter the temple of magic.

It does not really matter if you remember the right words of an incantation, and what you are supposed to use the ruby for, or what sage must be good to do; what matters is the caring that

happens between you and existence when you make yourself ready for magic and you pick up your tool.

In the end good magic is discovering that existence cares for you and nourishes, guides, and gives you clues and hints on your path.

Good magic is what happens when, for a while, you turn around and look at nature — and find her welcoming and wise, and ready to take you back — to take you home.

Acknowledgments

Martin Adam: 7 (left), 66, 67, 68, 69, 188, 195, 207, 228, 234/235, 237, 238,

A-Z COLLECTION: 138, 148

BRITISH MUSEUM: 57, 60, 182 (amethyst, red jaspers), 183 (whole page), 185 (diamond, amethystine agate, gold, silver), 201, 202, 205, 222/223, 224

DOVER – *Devils, Demons and Witchcraft* by Ernst and Johanna Lehner: 8/9, 13

IMAGES COLOR LIBRARY: 11, 232, 236

K & B FOTO – Massimo Borchi: 22

Bruno Kortenhorst: 7 (right), 31, 34, 36, 54 (air, water and earth), 122, 125, 127, 186, 198/199, 241

MACDONALD/ALDUS ARCHIVE: 24, 213, 218/219

PHOTOFILE: 250/251

SCIENCE PHOTO LIBRARY – John Sanford: 48 (both)
                                          – Robin Scagell: 49 (left)

Thomas von Solomon: 32/33

Jim Winkley: 46/47, 50/51, 113, 227, 244/245

ILLUSTRATIONS:

Alessandro Bartolozzi: 87, 129, 133, 146

Alessandro Beltramo: 144/145

Notes
Secrets
and Incantations

Notes Secrets and Incantations

Notes
Secrets
and Incantations

Notes
Secrets
and Incantations

Notes
Secrets
and Incantations